Silent Towns on the Prairie

AT RIGHT: *Truly a haunted house. Cobwebs are in every room, floors uneven and creaky, winds moan through the broken windows, doors hang loose, hinges need oil, the porch leans in a crazy fashion. It is not on the Hilton Hotel recommended list of good places to stay. You can't see the ghosts but you can feel them, the disembodied spirits, imagined or real, wandering around the rooms and haunting living things.*

LINDSAY WARD is the creator of the Dexter T. Rexter series as well as *Rosie: Stronger than Steel*, *This Book Is Gray*, *Brobarians*, *Rosco vs. the Baby*, and *The Importance of Being 3*. Her book *Please Bring Balloons* was also made into a play. Lindsay lives with her family in Peninsula, Ohio, where vehicles such as Scooper and Dumper take care of the roads all year round.

Silent Towns on the Prairie

North Dakota's Disappearing Towns and Farms

∽

by KEN C. BROVALD

LIBRARY OF CONGRESS CATALOG NUMBER:

ISBN: 1-57510-048-7

Pictorial Histories Publishing Co.
713 South Third Street West
Missoula, Montana 59801

Printed in Canada

Contents

~

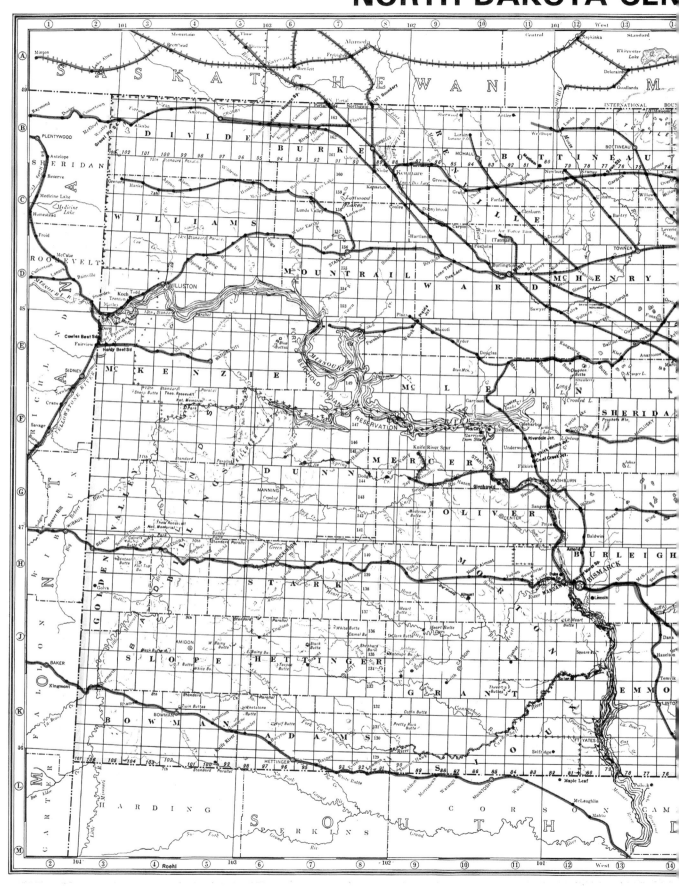

Published by the
**North Dakota
Public Service Commission**
January 1989
Commissioners
Dale V. Sandstrom
Bruce Hagen   Leo M. Reinbold

Burlington Northern RR	———
Soo Line RR	———
Red River Valley & Western RR	———
Canadian National RR	++++
Canadian Pacific RR	++++
Misc. & Short Line RR	++++
Time Zone Boundary	+++++++

Scale of Statute Miles

State Capital ⊛   County Seats ⊙

Dedicated to my parents, Arthur and Nettie Brovald,
who moved to the North Dakota prairie
when I was two years old.
Twelve of my happiest childhood years
were spent on this prairie land.

*"Ghosts take a particular shape, attached to certain legends
or superstitions. They are often considered premonitions or warnings.
They may appear in many forms and may manifest
themselves to any and all senses."*

Foreword

IF THE SILENT TOWNS of North Dakota could talk, the excitement of rural living would come rip roaring to life in more than 150 places. The tales they hold are just as fascinating as when the boardwalks echoed to the sound of heavy boots of a growing community. Isolated, one-industry towns (one grain elevator) and back road hamlets that once defined "country" are fading fast.

This writing is about the trials and tribulations of some of the small communities on the prairie. The rugged towns went about their business activities, never dreaming that within a generation or two they would be on the road to extinction. Sprouting up on the Great Plains, they grew slowly, and almost miraculously, the settlers and their progeny turned the heartland into a food and fiber breadbasket of the world, then began to walk the same pattern as the mighty buffalo— to near extinction.

My wife and I aimed to consider the state to see what binds these people who live here. What we found is that blood binds them. Second, third and even a fourth-generation people live on the land. It is what makes the state work and what makes them stay as long as they do.

This state, west of Minnesota and east of Montana, is the least visited state in the United States. Not many people come to North Dakota. With 2.9 million visitors, the state gets less visitor traffic than the outlet mall of L.L. Bean in Freeport, Maine. It is a place of sauerkraut and Danish pastry, of buffalo hot dogs and cowboy coffee, of lutefisk and lefse made from recipes hundreds of years old, of Sons of Norway dances. Lefse is a flat bread made from potatoes and flour, rolled thin as paper, baked, spread with butter and brown sugar or cinnamon, rolled up like a long cigar. Lutefisk, a form of bone dry cod fish, is soaked in a lye solution to break down the tough fibers. Water is changed every day for two weeks to leach out the lye, then the cod is boiled and finally smothered in melted butter. This traditional Norwegian food is a delight during the holiday season and on May 17, King Haakon I Day, the day of Norway's independence from Sweden and Denmark in 935 A.D.

This is a place of sunshine, where 100-degree heat, hailstones, and snow storms take their turn in predictable patterns.

The state is uncommercialized and is like a breath of fresh air. With our maps, notebooks, cameras, lens, film, and our misconceptions tucked firmly in place, we set out on a search for its history. We were looking for the bonding thread that led the pioneers to this land and made them stay. We started at the eastern border, in the Red River Valley. We were in the bread basket. The extraordinarily flat Red River Valley was left by the glacial Lake Agassiz, formed when the glaciers blocked the Red River, which spilled out over the land. It lay underwater for eons, and when the water disappeared it left a flat fertile valley. The Red River is like a giant serpent winding its way across the flat land. The river winds for 545 river miles, along the border with Minnesota, on an almost straight-line border of 210 miles.

When we saw a cluster of buildings on the horizon, with no water tower, and on a gravel road, we hit the brakes and traveled on it, whichever way it went, until we came to a disappearing (ghost) town. That is the wisdom of the neglected plains, and that is what we did for 15 eye-opening, tire-spinning days, traveling over 5,000 miles that mixed the bizarre with the beautiful. We could have traveled more miles and spent more days without leaving the state or breaking the spell. We traveled for miles and for hours, neither passing nor overtaking another car. The stillness was absolute and interrupted only by a two-cylinder John Deere tractor (a puttin' Johnny) working in a field or by the melodious songs of the birds.

As we drove around the countryside we sensed that the residents were talking about us. "See that guy over there with the camera? He's doin' a book about us." We traveled the back roads, where it was real "country," where roads had grass between the tire tracks. We enjoyed the quiet, and the brilliant twinkle of the stars, brighter and more numerous than we remembered from our childhoods. The early morning fragrance of the grasses, flowers and wheat fields was stimulating. The sights, sounds and scents have always been there, but driving through the state attuned our senses to the country.

The loss of the small town, of 'movin-on,' of being 'driven away' is not a modern phenomenon; it has been going on since the biblical times, since the time of Christ. Of all the talk of our "mobile society" almost no one seemed to know what lay down the road, virtually outside the front door. When we told a waitress in a small town that we were driving the length and width of the state, she asked if that meant going all the way to Kenmare, about 30 miles up the road. In our tour, we met very few people who grasped the unique charm of the state. North Dakota was our destination, but the journey was our reason. Each place is important to the people who still live there, and the prairie is important to history.

I have been influenced by friends passionate about subjects as diverse as coal mining, wheat farming, cattle ranching, railroad trains, celebrated buildings, rodeos, and ghost towns. We were seeking to photograph and document the remains of those enduring symbols of homestead life. In this quest, we traveled more than 5,000 miles on four occasions, visiting and photographing some 70 or more sites. The remains of these towns stand as a poignant memory of pioneer life on the prairie.

The towns looked empty, but the old buildings were crowded with memories, memories of thousands of people, young and old, rich and poor, family and friends, who worked, wed, went to war and came home again. The small town greeted them all; they were like a time machine.

Ghost towns are a novelty to someone who has lived most of their adult life in cities. In touring the plains states, I was struck by the number of dying communities. It was an eye-opener to see what was happening to rural America. A book on "what happened" is the result.

What is a ghost town? Surely it isn't the run-down old buildings, for they come and go. (I wish that more of them could have been saved.) Is it the people? They too come and go. No, it is something less tangible. It isn't the buildings, or the people, but the use to which they were collectively used. I am sad to see them go.

I really don't have a name for this journey. We both saw it in each and every resident, and you can see it in the photographs. The black and white photographs tell the story of the intertwining past, present and future. We wanted to capture the ghostly effect of the disappearing towns. The photographs made them look surrealistic. My passion is for the changing economic environment of small towns. Like an airplane taking off, the small town is fading farther and farther away.

In writing this book, we traveled the back roads, photographing the "graves," talking to the people who live there. Whenever the conversation turned to the town, it was in their eyes, we could feel it, we could see it in their faces. They all wanted a return to the better times and places. Their memories, always accurate but not always complete, were warm and glowing. This book is about some of the locations and points of interest.

Why North Dakota? It was not a "pick of the straw." On the Great Plains—from Canada to Mexico, from the Mississippi River to the Rocky Mountains—there are hundreds, if not thousands, of towns disappearing and becoming ghost towns. My roots are deep in the state. My growing up years were spent on a ranch/farm (we also grew wheat) in the northern part of the state. We knew the state and its people. The disappearing towns fascinated me, and captured the essence of something happening. The subject is too large to be a complete work but it records the legacy of some of these small towns that are disappearing and becoming ghost towns. I am not a historian. I'm a writer. I read, research, and write.

We had searched the back roads, poring over road maps, discovering the sites as if we were communicating with old friends. Like the man in the legend who is always looking for what is on the other side of the hill, we were drawn onward in the search for ghost towns. A person who roams the backroads is assumed to be lost, disoriented or suffering from too much sun. Some people went out of their way to question what we were doing and I think some even questioned our mental condition. To many people, most of the many ghost towns look very much alike, but to us, each one had its own individuality and personality.

We enjoyed many experiences while photographing the towns. We were startled by the deer, the antelope and prairie birds. We were overwhelmed by the beauty of the prairie sunsets, the expanse of the sky and the vast distances of the horizon. We were humbled by the realization that we were but a speck toiling across the face of the seemingly endless prairie. Only the true and dyed-in-the-wool researcher will visit the ghost towns. The photo opportunities are worthy of any calendar, but it requires hard work, commitment, and patience to find and take them.

While traveling the highways we recognized that we were following the early pioneer trails. United States Highway 85 follows the Marquis de Mores stage coach line from Medora to Dead-

wood. State highway No. 22 is the trail of the 60-mile Dickinson/Reeder stage line. Highways 24 and 1806 followed the early trail used by Indians and the military from the railhead at Mandan to the Fort Yates Indian Reservation. The ghosts of Custer and Sitting Bull, North Dakota's most famous son, still linger. The early trails changed the landscape and the culture. They are the arteries through which the blood of history flows.

I am drawn to the history of the rural towns and the stories they tell in their weathered walls and broken windows. I am curious about what happened to change the character of the land so dramatically in such a short period of time. I was transfixed by the flat, windswept prairie, where the constant winds manicure the golden fields of grain and the endless fields of grass are like a sea. We were moving through a time warp, as we exited from the past into the future.

The subject fascinated me and it captured the essence of something happening. The subject is too large to be contained in one book. North Dakota was selected. As we drove into, through and out of the small towns and into the real world, we felt the small towns folding behind us as we left. It is no small irony that during the period of America's greatest prosperity, in the decades following World War II, we destroyed the rural communities. We rejected the past and did little to embrace the future. The connection to the past and the future is the pathway that charms us. No one could predict that the rural population would be on the endangered list. But that is what happened. In the cauldron of changes, as the old order gives way, a new order emerges. The new order brought with it a technological revolution that continues to rage to this day. With the new century dawning, deterioration of small towns in rural America will escalate.

We visited every place shown in these photographs so the history is arranged and filtered through the camera lens. The lens of a camera is explicit. The shutter opened, then closed; my journey had begun. This writing is pieced together by gleaning historical books, poring through railroad timetables, road maps, newspaper clippings, making personal visits and lengthy tours of the state. Drinking coffee at local cafes and listening in on conversations, scribbling wildly in a notebook, all of this is included in my definition of history. This book sets to embark on a journey through the distant and not-to-distant past, to see and to document through an unforgettable season of change. In essence, the objective of this book parallels those of our mission, exploring North Dakota for an intimate look at a past life and a journey into the future, tracing the ties that bind the past to the future.

What I was after, was the "nugget" that tells me what kind of a state it is. That information came from talking with the people, photographs and an interest in the state. While the building and development of the early frontier is well documented, its demise is not given proper credit or consideration. This work is not intended to be a detailed study of the subject or a historical documentation of disappearing (ghost) towns; it is intended to be indicative of the dreams gained and lost as reflected by the dusty relics scattered across the landscape.

Introduction

THERE WAS A TIME when residents listened closely for the locomotive whistle and waited, on the platform, to greet and meet people and to see them off. From Crosby to Cando, from Fargo to Foxhome, from Grand Forks to Grafton, travel was by train. It was their gateway to and from the world, it was their prepaid ticket to the halls of the business world.

Life in the early villages centered around the railroad station. Things happened there. People came and left daily, and late news flashes were heard over the railroad telegraph. Newspapers, in most issues, carried a daily column advising that Mr. Jones or Miss Smith departed on No. 31. People didn't care much for fancy train names, they simply referred to them by number. The local railroad agent was the hero of the day, selling tickets, sorting freight and "reading" the telegraph. He was proudly known as Mr. Railroad.

Towns were spaced about eight to ten miles apart on the spine of a railroad. You could travel from one town to another, by horse and wagon, and be back in one day. The small towns were stepping stones on the prairie. The towns had all the services needed to live comfortably. There were schools, stores, churches, a grain elevator, hardware store, a depot, cafe, saloon, garage, a gasoline station, and a blacksmith who, with his hammer, anvil, and forge, pounded metal bars into horseshoes. But each passing year sees more of these businesses close and the small towns move closer to becoming ghost towns.

Roads were poor, in the early days, and weather was always a threat. The early cars were unreliable and were usually open air. Snow blocked the roads, and the towns were isolated for several days at a time. Travel of any distance was done by train, and you could get almost anywhere on the railroad. It was convenient and faster than a horse and the coach car was warmer than a wagon.

Hundreds of small towns were built on the prairie, and the new railroad connected them. Then they began to shrink. One by one, the towns began to lose business, then population. The schools closed, the stores went out of business, and people moved away and left only a smattering of residents. For two or three generations, the down-sizing of rural communities has taken place. It has shredded the fabric of American life and is changing the landscape. There is little chance that the trend can be reversed.

From 1870 to 1970 the small town was the heart of America. It was where the young grew up, went to school, married, raised a family, grew old and died, all in the same community. It nourished our civilization. World War II changed the small towns of America. Better automobiles and more of them and better highways and more of them, set the stage for the demise of the small towns.

Tales are still being told about the days when people came to town to pick up their mail, and buy groceries, then gather in the local cafe or bar to tell tales, exchange news, and gossip. But like the old towns the tall tale tellers are becoming more difficult to find. The grand old days are gone, but this book may renew a few memories as we travel the state in search of ghosts of the past.

It was a time of potbellied stoves, of kerosene lamps, of one-room schools, of home-canned foods, outdoor playgrounds and cemeteries. It stirs memories of the closing chapter in the settling and unsettling of the small prairie towns. What could have happened to these young, vibrant, thriving communities to cause their decline and bring them to where they are today? They had their day; they served their purpose. We are losing an irreplaceable chapter in our history with the abandonment of the small towns. A few rural communities still survive, but their numbers dwindle with each passing year.

The intrusion of electronic technology is everywhere. It is an instant reminder that we have traveled thousands of miles to experience and document the close of another chapter in North Dakota's history. While the efficiencies of computer communications are undeniable, the new order further dehumanizes society. For better or worse, the days of leanin' on the coffee counter listening to the locals, the timeless retreat of "hands on" interaction is over. Faceless electronics devices such as the Internet and e-mail are replacing the friendly chat at the post office or local coffee shop. We are drawn into a system that corrodes civic life, outlaws the human scale, defeats traditions and authenticity, and compounds our yearning for an everyday environment worthy of our affections.

The stone masons and bricklayers who built many of the buildings believed they would last forever, but sadly they have fallen into ruin. The buildings our predecessors constructed paid homage to history and they paid respect to the future in their sheer expectations that they would endure through the lifetimes of the people who built them.

The humming sound of these once viable communities is now but a cherished memory.

1

Disappearing Towns and Farms

GHOST TOWNS are usually associated with Old West towns abandoned when the mines played out. But there are ghost towns in many other places. More than 150 are found in North Dakota. Many people can tell stories of when these towns were booming.

A ghost town is defined as having 50 people or less. It is a shadow of its former self, for whatever reason, a community that is no longer able to support itself. All essential former activity has died or ceased, and those who remain must look to the county, the state or other communities to provide basic services, such as street maintenance, schools, fire and police protection. It is a town that has run its course of existence. The purpose for which it was founded has come to an end.

There is no reliable count of how many communities have vanished in recent decades because the Census Bureau does not monitor the status of towns with populations of less than 1,000, those most likely to disappear. Three hundred and seven North Dakota communities (83 percent) have less than 1,000 population and about one half of those have less than 50 inhabitants.

Ghost towns are a sagging tribute to our pioneering forefathers, and they live on in North Dakota. Some boast a few remnants, others have all but vanished. The pursuit of ghost towns can be likened to hunting for buried treasure. Their very elusiveness provides added elixir. Ghost towns reflect a desertion prompted when the railroads abandoned them, the highways passed them by and airlines flew over them.

We could find little information about the state. It was as if the omission of the state from the nation's archives was a cruel mistake, as if the place was an outback, a lost and forgotten place upon the far horizons of the country. The state is a large, square blank spot in the nation's mind. It has no common reference to the rest of the country. In architecture or geography it does not compare with the Chicago or New York skylines, or Florida's palm trees, or the forests of the West Coast. It is a small snapshot of waving wheat fields. The image that is held by most of the country is that North Dakota is a cold, isolated place.

The United States is unique, different from other developed countries in that schools, fire and police protection, and other essential services are paid by local taxes. When the people leave, they take their taxes with them and the entire infrastructure of the town collapses.

While the disintegration is often not pretty, there is frequently a certain elusive beauty to these ragged tattered buildings. Norway, LaMars, and Appam, with a population of one or two people and a barking dog, are probably the smallest towns in the state. Only a rare house or two and maybe an abandoned elevator remains. They have disappeared from the postal register and from highway maps. These sites probably never amounted to real towns but they have been persistent and refuse to completely die. To describe many of the "ghosts" is pointless, for the details vary little from town to town.

Many ghost towns are in areas of spectacular beauty. Some are raw and scarred, some yield excitement, some are rather mundane. But they all reflect something of the people who scratched out a hard living from a sometimes hostile land.

It is a paradox that there should be super markets, super malls, super centers and big box stores, super highways and super railroads, super cities, and super stars that are a part of America's burgeoning economic life, while there are no super ghost towns.

With the end of the Civil War, no force on earth could halt for long the number of troops and slaves who were now free to fight the Indians, to settle, to explore and to dig in the mines. With peace came massive unemployment and a restless nation.

During the early settlement period, the small towns were the gateway to the world. They were a quiet success story. They established themselves on the American landscape and preserved their ethnic heritage.

Most of the early towns were filthy. In the absence of sanitary facilities, refuse from butcher shops and garbage of every description was thrown in the street or out the back door. Herds of cattle and the domesticated horses added to the problem.

Personal cleanliness was no better. Few people took a bath. Most people slept in their clothes, and when winter roared in with considerable ferocity, new thicknesses of shirts and pants were added to keep warm. When summer came, the clothes were removed, layer by layer. Body lice were everywhere.

As a consequence, epidemics swept the towns. People died of tuberculosis, pneumonia, dysentery, and assorted skin infections. The cemetery was usually the first "site" on the frontier. It filled rapidly. When a church was built it was usually placed next to the already established cemetery.

Water was scarce. A water wagon was run from the nearest stream and its contents sold to the locals. Old whiskey barrels and later cisterns were used to collect rain water, for bathing and washing clothes. Many desperate people drank from this supply and caught typhoid fever and other waterborne diseases. Life was cheap and short.

The new towns were hardly picturesque. They consisted mostly of crude assortments of dugouts and tents in scattered disorder, some with blanket walls, sod roofs, potato-sack doors and windows. Under these conditions, most of the places we now call ghost towns were born and died.

Later, the tents were replaced with more permanent buildings, and when families arrived, the towns were cleaned up and rebuilt. The most popular item in the new house was a bathtub.

Some towns survived. Those that had a solid economic base and enjoyed a permanent population survived into this century. But many others became ghost towns when their economic base collapsed.

It was a place where you went to school, to a doctor, did business. It had a newspaper and stores, a railroad and a depot that served as the portal to the world for the people of the prairie plains. The small towns took what you had to sell (grain, livestock, eggs, milk, and cream); you brought back whatever you needed to buy. The small town had everything that was important to a community—people, information and products came and went through the small town.

2

The Making of North Dakota: A State is Born

IN THE EARLY 1800s, following the Louisiana Purchase, the territory west of the Mississippi River was awash in open territory, but little could be done to settle it. The West contained a billion acres of salable and unsettled land. For $15 million, an empire of 827,987 square miles of land was added, from the Mississippi River to the Rocky Mountains. Just about every description of the land west of the Alleghenies begins with the adjective "Great": The Great Lakes, Great Barrier, (the Alleghenies) Great Plains, Great Stony Mountains (later called the Rockies), Great Granary, Great Northern (railroad), Great Spirit, Great Chiefs (Sioux Indians), the Great Rivers—the Mississippi, (the father of waters), and the Missouri (big Muddy). They were the great gifts of Mother Nature.

We can thank Rene Robert Cavalier LaSalle, who discovered in 1682 which way the rivers ran. A great number of the settlers and the population today can trace their lineage deep into the Viking origins. The Vikings were classic explorers and conquerors, who pushed the frontier westward. Bold, adventurers, ferocious warriors, these people were well suited to settle the prairie. They left a mark on the state's history that is indelible to this day.

The early settlers entered the sparsely populated territory with little money to tame and harness this land. There were thousands of square miles of uncharted wilderness. There was no tech-nological base, no economic base, no significant internal transportation.

From the headwaters of the Red River at Wahpeton to its end point at Lake Winnipeg there is a subtle drop in elevation of only 233 feet in 545 river miles. The valley slopes just as slightly from its edge to the center. It is as flat as a billiard table and just as green.

The Great Plains were elusive, a relatively un-definable line that constantly retreated westward as population pushed it further into the frontier. Settlers were baffled as to the exact location—it was found somewhere between civilization and savagery. Easterners who viewed this phenomenon from afar, and Westerners, who thought they lived on or near the magic line, were equally unable to give it a definite geographical location.

The Great Plains were Mother Nature's great gift. Blessed with favorable climate and fertile soil, Mother Nature has been very generous in providing for the needs of the human race, but with the perversity usually associated with the female gender, she rarely put these gifts where humankind wants them to be, thus the need for transportation. There are only three basic human activities—growing things, making things and moving things.

The territory had to be tamed. Divided by rivers that ran the wrong direction, the internal transportation system was inadequate in the immense territory. The Great Rivers—the Red, the Missouri, the Yellowstone—all had a long way to go to reach the markets. The Missouri River was the only true navigable river. The Red River did not go to the right places, and the water level did not permit year around use. They were splendid for fur traders, but of little use for efficient transportation.

The land contained rich deposits of coal and oil, and immense acres of rich top soil. If settlers could conquer the twin problem of isolation and distance, the land could be settled. The solution turned out to be a Rail Road (two words at the beginning).

A typical wagon carried a load of 6,000 pounds, but some carried a 10,000 pound load, or a "hundred-hundred" as old time wagoneers liked to boast. Wheels were round and flat, and all this weight met the road in tiny areas and pounded the road into atoms. Freight wagons frequently had 8-inch wide rims, they were easier on the road bed, stage coaches usually had four inch rims, or less, which cut the road bed to pieces. Damage to the road beds was enormous. Stage and wagon routes were mostly west or south bound, (military freight and mining material to Montana and the Black Hills).

Movement upgrade was agonizingly slow, the trek was based on four-legged horsepower, not steam locomotives, which came ten years later. Downgrade was equally slow for reasons of terror. The braking system was simple. Get the horses to stop and the wagon would stop. This frequently caused an accident, for the heavy wagon rolled into the horses, causing injury or broken legs. A pole through a wheel usually pulled the wagon to one side or broke the spokes. Help and repairs could be miles and hours away. A rock or log was often carried on the rear of the wagon to be dragged behind to slow it on a downgrade. This was not too effective because it added weight to the wagon when on the level or going uphill. A brake rubbing block against the rim was not very effective either—not enough pressure could be applied by the driver. Early stages had travel classes. On hilly runs and creek crossings, first class passengers stayed in the carriage, while second class walked and third class pushed or braked going downhill.

The braking system was not good enough in the rolling hills and mountains. Going uphill is a matter of economics—apply enough horsepower and you will get to the top. Going downhill is a different matter—it's a matter of survival. When a wagon went out of control, the downhill trip was even more exciting than usual. On a ten percent grade or on a rainy day, the wagon slipped out of control because the drivers could not rely on such a braking system. The gravity coin has two sides, and gravity has no friends.

By the mid 1800s as many as 1,200 to 1,500 Red River carts per year were plying between the buffalo killing fields of central North Dakota and St. Paul, carrying buffalo hides and prepared buffalo meat. Red River carts were a two-wheeled contraption built entirely of wood, which squealed so loudly, as the wheels rolled on wooden axles, that it is said that a caravan of them could be heard for miles. They were not too successful.

Men became interested in creating a roadbed that could carry a heavier load—a road of rails. A single horse pulling a load on rails could equal the hauling capacity of 12 horses on a turnpike. Steam power would increase the carrying capacity by tenfold or more. A railroad would change that. Freight and people could and would travel in either direction with ease. Livestock and grain could be marketed; people had better communications with the world.

The Great Missouri River was the spine of the vast territory. The downstream commerce was mostly furs and buffalo hides, while upstream cargo was military goods, foodstuffs, whiskey, moving mostly in flat boats, slowly and only in the summer months. The keel boats had to contend with the "ornery river." A typical boat carried fifty tons, requiring seven to ten men, traveling about four miles an hour. Mother Nature's great gifts were in the river systems, which contributed greatly to the transportation stew.

The Sioux, Hidatsa, Arikaras and Mandan Indians farmed the rich farmlands of the Missouri River valleys since the 13th century. The Indians lived in the way of progress and some conflict was inevitable. There was an instant enchantment with violence and a compulsion for a quick and final physical showdown. Few of the intruders respected the right of the red man.

We followed their trails, studied their teepee rings, their burial grounds and the buffalo wallows. They lost it all when the white settlers moved in.

Civilization was bound to the river fronts (Red River and Missouri), but the rivers did little to develop the state. The rivers ran in the wrong direction. There were a few trading and military posts along the rivers, but there was little development in the interior. It was a mysterious and distant place. Geographically connected to no one, it was virtually exiled from the affairs of the rest of the nation by the "tyranny of distance." The distance is still there, but it has been tamed.

Development and settlement was slow. The early wagon trains and pioneers skipped over the state reaching for the gold fields of Montana and Idaho. Gold and silver ore was dug out of the mountains, and after smelting could be carried out in a saddle bag. Ore, in its raw form, is worthless. It needs the services of a gold smelter, which gave rise to gold stage robberies. No thieves ever robbed an ore wagon, no one rode shotgun. Thieves wanted only the finished product. Important as it was before the turn of the century, gold mining is a short-lived enterprise. An underground seam of gold or silver can only be taken out once. With the passage of time, all gold deposits are destined for exhaustion.

The great prairie had no such riches to attract the rough element. Settlers had to grow their own wheat, which could not be carried on the back of a horse. Gold and silver would not nor could not sustain Montana or Idaho. Count the number of failed gold camps. One early pioneer was said to remark, "We skipped over paradise and landed in hell." Wheat would sustain North Dakota for more than a century, and it still does.

On May 20, 1862, President Lincoln penned his name at the bottom of a historical and far reaching legislation. This was the enormously significant Homestead Act, a law that made millions of Americans into property owners for the first time. The act offered the promise of free parcels of public land to citizens over 21 who cleared, improved and lived on that land for three years or longer. During the late 19th and early 20th centuries, thousands of homesteaders rushed into the west. The population of North Dakota increased dramatically, in the 50-year period from 1870 to 1920, the population went from 2,500 white people to about 650,000. All homesteaders and early towns struggled to carve out a place on the map. Some succeeded, many didn't. Some succeeded well into the 1930s when the Depression and drought conspired to devastate them.

The peak in the homestead grants in the Dakota's was reached in 1884, when 11,083,000 acres were granted to settlers. The population of the two Dakota's reached 559,583. To a people whose ancestors had only recently been peasants in Europe, owning a patch of land was not only seen as a path to wealth, but more important, as the sole guarantee to freedom. They could not believe that America was so rich it could give land away.

DEDICATED TO NORTH DAKOTA PIONEERS

How exciting an adventure it must have been,
not knowing how or when to begin.
Wagon wheels were frozen fast in their track,
with no hope of movin' 'till spring comes back.

And the cold, oh the cold, it stabbed like a knife,
through a crack in the wall and a shivering wife.
It was a long way from Norway to their new land,
through their faith in God did they withstand.

They wondered to a strange and distant land,
on the great prairie they came to understand.
The new land welcomed the ethnic brew,
she promised refuge to the hapless crew.

The first came in groups of four, then five,
it was a struggle to keep them alive.
Each spring they came by the score,
Land was whipped to feed more and more.

Farms were settled in a few years,
by their brawn and a river of fears.
Wrestling the land into a state,
that was their purpose; that was their fate.

(composed by the author)

The Civil War was winding down and would end in the foreseeable future, the fraternity of army officers needed to find a place of occupation for its decreasing ranks. General Alfred Sully accepted the assignment to lead an Indian campaign on a "special visit" to some of the tribes. It would establish his reputation as an Indian fighter. He went forth into Indian country to do his duty—to kill Indians. General Sully and 2,000 cavalry men fought the bloodiest battle ever fought in North Dakota. The Battle of Whitestone Hills, near Jamestown in 1863, cost Sully 22 men. Fifty were wounded, and 300 Indians died. In 1864, Sully engaged a large band of Sioux in the Killdeer Mountains (place where they kill); the Indians retreated to the Little Missouri Badlands country, Sully followed. Water was scarce, rainfall is about 12 inches a year, but Sully's troops found water and named the spot Sully Springs. General Sully called the badlands, "hell with the fires out." He found that the quality of life deteriorated geometrically with the miles traveled into the region. Sully came upon a large band of Sioux at the east edge of the badlands, an estimated camp of 1,600 lodges, with 5,000 to 6,000 warriors, against his force of 2,200 troopers. The Indians were routed, the camp destroyed.

Notwithstanding Lieutenant Colonel George Armstrong Custer, General Alfred Sully was an Indian fighter without equal. He accomplished the task of making the state safe for settlers. He transformed the land from a hostile land to one where peaceful settlements were made. The campaign severely affected Sully's rheumatism near the heart. He spent the winter of 1864–65 in Sioux City, Iowa. He returned to North Dakota in the spring of 1865 to continue his campaign. Ghosts of General Sully and his 2,200 troops can be felt, the war cry of the Sioux can still be heard, if you listen to the wind.

Usually, the Indians avoided attacking an organized army, choosing instead a "hit and run" strategy, which was immensely successful. Some historians tell us that the Indians lost all the battles. This is not true. They won more than they lost. They were fierce, cunning and smart fighters. In general, when forces were equal, the Indian won his war. They fought hard but lost the last battle and with it, their cause. In general, Indians efforts suffered from lack of coordination and a failure of the tribes to cooperate. They were beaten by technology—the telegraph, the railroad, repeating rifles—and most important, by the destruction of their food supply, the buffalo.

The Indians had been corralled and placed in reservations; the Red River and Missouri River boats were gone, as were the fur traders, trappers, and the frontier men with their rifles. Their ghosts followed the buffalo and Indian trails. Except for a few white settlers, the region was totally empty, unsettled and uninhabited. It was a land in waiting; North Dakota's time had come. Transportation costs were prohibitive, as much as $1 a ton per mile. Any haul by horse and wagon over ten miles ate up profits quickly. North Dakota needed railroads and settlers. It needed people, the right kind of people, to match the prairie. After the surrender at Appomattox, the boom was on.

The Northern Pacific Railway (NP) had been chartered in 1864, before the Civil War's end, but the man on the street did not believe that this route was a viable enterprise. To most people, this land was looked upon as the land of the Sioux, which, in fact, it was. The Great Plains were still considered desert to be crossed, not settled. The wisdom of constructing 1,800 miles of track through uninhabited country was questioned. The argument continued for years that the railroad was a military necessity and essential for internal development.

The rail line now threatened to become a reality as survey crews took to the field and planted survey stakes across the barren sod. The route of the "iron horse" would point directly into the heart of Sioux land. The NP was on its way west and only the Panic of 1873 would blunt its forward thrust as it reached the new village of Bismarck. Even the Indians knew this was but a pause, not a termination. Two years after it was completed, the NP did, by itself, solve the "Great Sioux" problem." The telegraph and railroad made it possible to transfer information, men and supplies quickly to where they were needed.

The gold, silver, and copper strikes in Montana created additional excitement. There was a rising demand for heavy machinery for use in the lode mining. The river systems were woefully inadequate to supply the growing demand for supplies and overland wagons were no better than river hauling. It would require a more efficient mode of transportation than land vehicles could offer.

The upper reaches of the Missouri River were not considered agriculturally desirable and there was little reason for farmers to look in that direction when they sought to take advantage of the new Homestead Act. Generally, none of the veterans who served in the Indian campaigns and who had struggled through the badlands, had any inclination to return as settlers.

The greatest catalyst to the development of the state occurred in 1871, when the NP crossed the Red River at what is now Fargo, and streaked across the state to the Missouri River, reaching there in 1873. The nearest settlement was 771 miles away, at Bozeman, Montana. Along the entire line, there was not a sign of civilization. The prospect for the future was very bleak. It was not encouraging.

"Only 25 miles to go, only 15 miles, only 10 miles and only 5 miles to the Missouri River" was the chant of the construction workers. They had overcome the Indian, disease, weather, isolation and hard work. Weary men and machines had accomplished the impossible. They had conquered the twisting tumbling unconquerable West. The two rivers were joined. They had 577 miles to go to Bozeman. The toughest construction task was just ahead, the badlands, which would require much heavy cutting for about 100 miles.

For workers laying track on the NP, home consisted of train cars fitted with bunks. Food and other supplies were needed for survival in the harsh environment. In the newly established railroad construction camps, small clusters of buildings were built, and as the track slowly moved westward, some of the buildings were taken down and moved to the next construction camp. Other buildings were not worth moving and were left to become a basis for a town site. To provide for the workers as they worked their way west farther and farther from white civilization, a work train was developed that closely resembled the hospital trains of the Civil War. They provided bunks, kitchens, hospital care, and supplies. They moved west with the work force, over the newly laid track. They were self-sufficient, small towns on wheels. The train also served as a center of civilized order in an environment that often did not even provide shade for the laborers.

As the "iron horse" moved westward, about a dozen cars were attached, each one designed for a special purpose. Cars were filled with tools; one car was a blacksmith shop, another a carpenter car, and several flat cars loaded with rail, ties, spikes, and other road building materials. It was an army, which developed into a society of its own, on the moving frontier. When the work trains moved on, they left settlements in the middle of nowhere, settlements that had no legal or economic security beyond the railroad. The settlements attracted anyone in search of wealth, including Indians, settlers, miners, ranchers, former slaves, storekeepers, and gunfighters, all of diverse backgrounds. Before 1890, outlaws, gamblers, ladies of the night, hoboes and other wanderers outside the bounds of the law saw the gradual reduction in wilderness as more land went into private hands.

Easterners and soldiers viewed the railroad workers, settlers and Indians as cultural curiosities and worth the trip, and then they went home with fascinating tales to tell of the "wild" west. Passengers were curious and fascinated by the forts and their inhabitants. Here was a chance to see a live American Indian, more or less in captivity, and to write about it. Passengers would remark about the blankets, face paint and the customs of the Indian.

Easterners and Civil War officers tried to control the workers by military discipline. It didn't work; military rule failed on the frontier. Newly freed soldiers and slaves would have little to do with military rule. They laughed at the officers. Order would be brought to the frontier by civil law, not by military rule.

Former slaves and Civil War veterans got jobs working on the Northern Pacific. Those who didn't gathered and sold buffalo bones and hides and shipped them east from the new rail head at Dickinson. There was a demand for buffalo tongues, considered a delicacy for the elite. Buffalo were killed just for their tongues, leaving the remaining meat to decay. Pickled in brine and sold for 25 cents at the local trading post, the tongues were then shipped downstream to St. Louis. Hundreds of thousands of the mangy shaggy animals died, killed by white and Indian hunters, for the single purpose of yielding four pounds of its total weight.

Most rivers in the eastern part of the state ran north and south at right angles to the railroad, while those in the west flowed west and east, parallel to the rail line. The Heart River, near Mandan, was crossed six times in five miles, and the Sweet Briar River, which winds snakelike across the foothills, was crossed 27 times in eight miles. Crossing the badlands was costly. Many trestles were built, and heavy embankments were cut to build a roadbed. Before the line was completed, a sum of $3,500,000 was spent, a huge sum in the 1870s. The construction crews were 152 miles west of Mandan. New Salem, Glen Ullin, Richardton, Gladstone, Dickinson, and Belfield came into existence in the late 1870s, laid out by the NP Land Department, primarily as service stations for the railroad, side tracks, water and fuel facilities, and the like.

Despite the enthusiasm of its promoters, progress was slow, made more difficult by the stubborn terrain, and lack of population. Only 2,500 white people could be counted in 1870, when the NP entered the state, and only 36,900

ten years later. The population increased to 648,872 in 1920 and remains substantially the same in 1990, at 652,695.

Most people think that when the NP was completed across the United States that it was finished, but it wasn't. There wasn't enough freight business to make the line viable and there was no local passenger business. The NP needed settlers to survive. Branch lines were built like spider webs, and immigrants were brought in to settle the land and generate the needed business. Early railroad builders called these lines expansion lines, settlement lines, grain gathering lines, feeder lines and finally just simply branch lines.

Regular train operations began in 1871, making the NP and North Dakota an accomplished fact. Except for a few interruptions due to floods or snow storms, the trains have run continuously ever since.

The flat plains have nourished a civilization for 700 years. The early Indians and later the settlers shaped the state. By the mid-1800s, settlers began moving in. They were chafing under a military yoke and political appointees. On March 12, 1802, the first non-Indian child, a girl, was born at Pembina, a British built military/fur trading post among the Chippewa Indians, to Pierre Bonza and his wife who were Negroes.

Upon arriving in the territory in 1861, the first territorial governor, Dr. William Jaynes, counted only 76 non Indians living in the territory. By the time of statehood, 28 years later, there was sufficient population to become a state. Dozens of military forts were established, mostly along the rivers, but they did little to develop the state. The early settlers began to demand independence. They wanted a railroad, which they got in 1871, and statehood, which came in 1889. Enter now the NP, the Great Northern (GN), and the Minneapolis, St. Paul & Sault Ste Marie (SOO LINE), and the stirring account of the making of a state. Any student of North Dakota history cannot avoid the conclusion that the contribution of the railroads, was and still is awesome.

Dakota Territory, in its first 28 years of existence, was treated like a colony by a dictatorial congress and a gaggle of feisty politicians, which exercised absolute control over all the hapless territory. The climax to the game of territory control was that the "Yankton Ring" elected a squatter legislature, a governor, and territorial delegates to congress. Ballot boxes were stuffed to ensure that Yankton would be the territorial capital. The politicians were often corrupt and uninformed about the territory. The Northern Pacific Railway (NP) believed, as did the politicians, that Dakota should remain a Territory, that a strong state government undoubtedly would try to exert more control over its railroad activities.

Bismarck, then a small town, was selected to be the new capital. The NP donated 160 acres of land of which the state building still stands. The first governor's office was in a railroad car, "a capitol on wheels." The new city raised $100,000 for the new capitol and almost went bankrupt. A few minutes before midnight, on November 2, 1889, newly elected Governor John Miller, a non-politician, proclaimed statehood. He was manager of a 27,000-acre "bonanza" wheat farm in the Red River Valley. The state was now simultaneously liberated from the "Yankton Ring" and released from unscrupulous politicians. The cornerstone celebration was combined with special events, including four special Northern Pacific trains, carrying such dignitaries as former President Ulysses S. Grant; Marshall Field, the Chicago giant retailer; and Jim Hill, the giant of the Great Northern Railway.

Although tired of almost three decades of struggles to attain statehood, citizens had the energy to celebrate. With the electrifying news that "we are a State," they hopped, skipped, and jumped up and down with glee, from border to border, from river to river, around every curve and loop. As the cavalcade unwound, the crowd displayed a wild enthusiasm, with people of all ages waving flags and blowing horns in a half-mile parade, (difficult to assemble in the small town), ablaze with torches and fireworks, beneath a canopy of smoke and noise. North Dakota was no longer a settlement frontier. It was joined by other states to form a continuous line of states from coast to coast and north to south. By the end of the 1800s, the settlers had earned a place in United States history and it all happened in a 30-year period, after the NP crossed into the territory in 1871.

After the Civil War, a new era of intensive railroad building began. Thousands of young men found themselves disgorged into a changing world. Union and Confederate survivors, former slaves, farm boys, immigrants, and itinerants—all were searching for their dreams of adventure, wealth, and fame. Most thought they would find it, "workin' on the railroad" that was winding its way across the continent to the Pacific. Life in the construction camps was cheap. Workers suffered intolerably long hours, unfit food and infected beds. During unhealthy "rest" periods, booze, gambling, wrenching, and brawling were the favorite pastimes.

The Union Pacific and Central Pacific had been joined in Utah on May 10, 1869, where a gold spike was dropped into a prepared hole on which was inscribed this prayer, "May God continue this unity of our country as this Railroad unites the two great Oceans of the world." Despite the inscription on the head of a spike, God seemed to be ticketless as the NP tracks stretched from coast to coast in this spiritual wasteland.

One element was absent: there were no churches on the "Hell on Wheels." What the new settlers found were canvas tents, plain board shanties, or turf hovels, left by the grand movement of the railroad. Restaurant and saloon keepers, gamblers, outlaws running from the law, desperadoes of every grade—the vilest of men and women followed the construction camps.

No era in United States history was more fascinating than the taming of the West. Movies, television and writers have glorified the violence of the taming, but there was, as well, a more gentle, less dramatic influence: the church. During the pioneer days, the rural areas had not built enough large buildings to sustain all the services needed. One such need was churches. Few churches had been established, and no building could accommodate even the smallest congregation. The people depended on traveling circuit riders, on horseback, with bibles hung around their necks, holding meetings in tents.

A most unique influence on settling the communities along the railroad was the railroad coach "chapel car." Rev. Boston Smith, a Baptist minister, recognized the need to bring religion to the sparse settlements. Smith feared that he would lose the congregations established by circuit riders unless something was done to keep them together. Across the state, Rev. Smith found four great railroads stretching across the prairie: The Northern Pacific; St. Paul, Minneapolis and Manitoba; Milwaukee and St. Paul; and the SOO Line, with feeder lines thrown out in every direction. He noted that there were about 4,000 miles of rail lines in the state and that a large number of small hamlets dotted the countryside at frequent intervals. Such settlements contained no schools, no churches, and no buildings sufficiently large to hold more than twenty people. He reasoned that a "Hell on wheels" should be challenged with the "church on wheels."

In mid-1890, he approached General Manager William S. Mellen, of the Northern Pacific, in Minneapolis, with a novel idea: a traveling church on wheels. With winter coming on, he could not hold meetings in tents. The NP responded immediately by providing a free coach and free transfer from one small community to the next. Rev. Smith had his church on wheels.

The first car was named "Evangel." Its ministry covered 70,000 square miles of villages along the railroads. General Manager Mellen issued instructions to the officers: "You will pass Mr. Boston Smith and one attendant with chapel car over our lines. You will arrange to take the car on any train he desires, you will sidetrack it wherever he wishes. Make it as pleasant for Mr. Smith as you can." The cars were placed at a convenient point for the comfort and easy access of the people in the town. Usually this was near the depot.

Historic events are recognized in retrospect and often too late. What began as an effort to satisfy spiritual needs to early settlers grew into a nationwide crusade. Seven churches-on-wheels were built and used. Most of the cars were 75 feet long, and were designed with living quarters for the minister

and his family and seating for as many as 100 worshipers. People traveled many miles, in all kinds of weather, for the rare opportunity to attend a church meeting. They came on horseback, by wagon and some walked. One man rode a steer. Another man in North Dakota walked nine miles in each direction in sub-zero weather to attend a meeting. Many immigrants could not speak nor understand the English language. Some missionaries in the chapel cars ministered to Danes, Norwegians, Swedes and Germans in their own language.

The primary function of the NP and other railroads was to haul the goods of commerce. The trackage in the towns was not built with chapel cars in mind. Side-tracking the cars for days, weeks and even months often conflicted with the railroad's need to use the trackage for commercial purposes. It was finally agreed to build a special spur track at selected locations. It cost $8 to build a 100-foot spur, and often the missionaries helped build the track.

The tracks were thereafter known, in most communities, as the chapel car track. New Salem, west of Bismarck, was chosen as one of the selected locations, as were Casselton, Valley City, Jamestown, and Bismarck. There were others in scattered locations.

One young man, upon seeing a "church" car remarked, "I've 'saw' a cattle car, a hog car, a freight car, a passenger car, a smoking car, a baggage car and a sleeping car, but I 'ain't' never 'saw' a church car. If that don't beat the devil." That was just what the "church car" was designed to do.

The bishops personally kept the cars clean. They swept it, cleaned the lamps, washed the windows, and played the organ. The cars were heated by wood or coal. Each of the cars were gifted with the Estey pump organ by Col. J.J. Esty of Vermont and Thomas Edison gave the first six chapel cars one of his famous phonographs.

No work was allowed on the Sabbath and no drinking or gambling establishments were allowed to dissipate the men's morals. Abstinence and celibacy weighed heavily on the minds of the bachelor workers. Men outnumbered women by 30 to one. Some of the men were devout Christians, but many were not. Some had not been to a church service in years. There is no question that the chapel car ministry did much for the railroad and its men.

Many of the townspeople were not receptive to the chapel car ministry. One car was covered by a barrage of eggs and another was covered with red paint. The car "Glad Tiding" was almost destroyed by fire. Someone had set fire to brush along the side-track where the car was placed. Through the heroic efforts of the local people the car was saved. Acceptance by other denominations was not an automatic thing, and the church car was publicly denounced by other churches. The missionaries were appalled to think that anyone would go to such lengths of disapproval. The "Glad Tiding" last served in Flagstaff, Arizona.

All religions using the chapel cars faced fire, drought, heat, cold, sandstorms, tornadoes, fatigue, isolation, hostiles, the Mormons, the Ku Klux Klan and town toughs. Protestants and Catholics usually at odds on many issues joined forces to bring the chapel cars to the frontier.

By 1942, the effectiveness of a traveling church car was in question. The need for missionaries in the communities was past. The service was discontinued for logical reasons. There were no new frontiers to conquer, the Second World War was on, the automobile had ended the isolation, churches had been established in most towns and the day of free railroad passage was past. The relationship between Smith and the NP lasted 52 years.

As early as 1914, the railroads began to charge from five to 56 cents a mile to move the cars. Then in 1917 the Government took over operations of the railroads, and a new regulation was enforced forbidding free transportation for all private cars, which included cars used for religious purposes. Following the end of World War I, the Interstate Commerce Commission (ICC) banned the use of wooden passenger cars for safety reasons. This new regulation severely restricted the mobility of the church cars. There were considerable problems moving from one location to another. Most of the cars, except the last two, were wooden.

The contribution made by the NP was significant. The achievements and contributions made to the communities were enormous. By 1905, the chapel car ministry had established 135 churches, and many function today because of the vision of Rev. Smith. Though the chapel car era ended long ago, there will never be an end to its influence. The chapel car, the missionaries and the railroad formed an unusual partnership that made it all possible. Free passage of chapel cars, until 1914, greatly reduced the cost of operations. Without that gift, there probably never would have been a church car ministry. It is a unique and beautiful page of history, and well worth remembering.

The first car, the "Evangel," was sold in 1901 for $1,000 to pay off the mortgage on the bishop's house. For a while, after retirement, the car was stationed in Carrington, North Dakota, It served as a chapel at the mission and was finally dismantled.

The "Emmanual" held its church car's last service in Del Norte, Colorado, in 1942. The car was moved to Swan Lake Campground at Viborg, South Dakota, near Yankton, South Dakota, then to a storage yard (junk yard) in Sioux Falls, South Dakota, where it rusted, was partly dismantled, and allowed to deteriorate for 20 years. The remains were rescued and moved to the Prairie Village Historical Park near Madison, South Dakota, in 1972. It is being restored by including replicas of the wooden pews, new alter, a brass lectern, a study at one end and bookshelves to the ceiling: Other refurbishing includes seating of three on one side of the aisle and two on the other, and an Espy organ at the alter end. It is now on the National Register of Historic Places, which qualifies it for federal restoring funds. Some $3400 has been spent on this project. It was the last car in the "steel apostle" fleet services, and one of the only three remaining.

We studied the railroad track layouts in some towns, looking for evidence of the "chapel car church tracks." We found none; all had been removed long ago and no one seemed to know anything about them. Some old timer remembered, but they all said it was a long time ago, before the war. Younger people had a strange look when asked about the early church cars and churches.

The presence of Rev. Boston Smith and his counterparts—Episcopal Bishop William. D. Walker, Baptist Dr. Wayland Hoyt of Minneapolis and Catholic Archdeacon Father Francis Clement Kelly—is very strong in the small town churches. Did they walk these streets or hold services in chapel cars in this town?

Churches exerted a strong influence on life in North Dakota. Total present membership is about 485,000, 71 percent of the population, the highest ratio in the nation. The membership includes 216,000 Lutherans, 171,000 Catholics, 27,000 Methodists and 14,000 Baptists. In all there are nearly 50 denominations in the state, with a total of 1,678 churches. With the declining town and farm population, many churches have closed or joined with other congregations in nearby towns.

Forty town sites were established by the NP on the main line of the first railroad in North Dakota. One hundred years later, 14 of these sites are ghost towns. They passed into the role of a passing track for the trains. Spiritwood, Sterling, Cleveland, Fryburg and Sully Springs had hopes of making it in the business world. They were on the main line of a transcontinental railroad. They were in new territory, starting from nothing; they had only one way to go—to grow. They could not fail, but they did. Like most towns they came into existence because they were needed as a siding track for the railroad. Half a dozen dilapidated buildings are scattered here and there. Old brick schools, which have become the victims of vandalism, and abandoned churches are about all that is left of these little towns. In some, there is no evidence that there was even a town. The communities went from open prairie to a town and back to open prairie in 50 or more years. Their birth and death has largely to do with the railroad. Railroad deregulation and the abolishment of the Interstate Commerce Commission, which regulated grain rates, the entire grain transportation infrastructure

changed, and it hurt the rural communities.

North and South Dakota were admitted into the Union in an act signed by President Benjamin Harrison on November 2, 1889. It had been a territory for 28 years. North Dakota had been admitted to the Union as the 39th state, sharing its admission with South Dakota. The two states still dispute who was admitted first.

The much disputed boundary was established on the 46th parallel, which was marked with 800-pound stone monuments, eight feet long, ten inches square, with North Dakota chiseled on one side and South Dakota on the other, with an "M" on the east side to indicate the mileage from its starting point . They were set one-half mile apart. The boundary is 361.5 miles long, extending from the Bois de Sioux River on the Minnesota border to the Montana border. It is the longest such border marker in the nation. There were 720 markers. Most are still in place, although some have been removed or destroyed to build a road on the state border. Some were destroyed by farm machinery. They guard the border like "silent sentinels" of the prairie.

The expanding settlements created hundreds of towns and buildings in the last century for a particular function and when that function changed, the towns had to change, too. America's population has shifted quickly from an agricultural nation to high technology, from rural to urban life, with the increasingly larger number of people living in the most populous municipalities. The people moved away from using the train for transportation to using the automobile.

It wasn't long before the elements of time, distance and technology had overtaken the prairie villages and left them as ghost towns. The decline of these towns began with the changing needs of the world's economy. The growth of the small town is the story of westward expansion, the story of the nation's economic development and a singular factor in the rapid rise of American industry. It was only reasonable to expect that the towns would mirror this trend, away from the mainstream of America.

3

Wheat and Cattle Country: Heartland of America

THIS IS AN AGRICULTURAL STATE, as it has been for more than 100 years. It is dedicated to corn, wheat, soybeans, potatoes, sugar beets and cattle, all in wholesale quantities. The sky is an ocean of blue and the wheat fields are a sea of gold. It was wheat by the wagon load, a wheat bonanza.

The Peace Garden State, with a population about equal to Oklahoma City, had only eight homicides in 1995, the lowest murder rate in the nation. Its residents pointed out the fundamental health and stability of their society. Something like 85 percent of the students come from two-parent families. Divorce is below the national average, so is the percentage of births to unmarried women. The high school graduation rate is always near the top, 87 percent, and the economy is strong, with less than three percent of workers unemployed. Some 73 percent of the population was born in the state. Such conformity may hinder social diversity but it sure contributes to social stability. Few people leave family and friends behind, then regret and suffer for it later.

The state has always been somewhat handicapped because no one, not even the residents, can decide if it's quite Midwest or West. The reason for the confusion is that it is both. The Missouri River divides the East from the West and is the dividing line between two climates, two cultures, two ways of life and topographies. The river is the great divide where the West begins. The Missouri River is like a giant artery running through the heart of the Dakotas.

Massive power lines march across the landscape, carrying electricity from power dams on the Missouri River. Be alert for slow moving farm vehicles, or the rare highballing eighteen wheeler, in the short rolling hills. A wide load can fill the entire road, leaving only the narrow shoulder or the ditch for other travelers. Roads tend to be straight, then suddenly you "hang a hard right" and unwary travelers can be fatally surprised by ninety-degree turns. Slow down! Drivers of nearly all farm vehicles will wave, but watch out for immense farm machinery, which have the right-of-way. Some farmers do not fence their fields on the sensible theory that wheat does not escape, but they do turn their cattle onto the fields after harvest, so watch for cattle grazing in the ditches. A sudden noise can send them rushing into the road, catching an unwary motorist off-guard.

Pack a lunch. Many "towns" have neither gas stations nor cafes. The local church may encourage togetherness, and farmers may gather to gossip at a local coffee shop, but modern times find local residents driving to larger cities for shopping at malls. Without enough business, the cafe, which used to be the town's crossroads, was replaced by a "corner" offering gasoline, a few groceries and necessities tucked away in the shelves.

Like their neighbors in the farm belt, the residents are a little confused about their role and position in the modern world. Traditional agriculture, once the state's economic basis, is changing. Farms are bigger and the father can only hand down one farm. The younger members of the family, who once stayed to work the family farm, now follow their parents' advice and leave the state for higher education. Most don't return. If they do, they return as urban professionals. The wishful thinking that people would return to their "roots" is not happening.

Farmers have steadily acquired more land, more machinery and bigger mortgages. Deserted farmsteads outnumber inhabited ones and the countryside is dotted with the wreckage of abandoned towns and farms. During the 1995–1997 crop years, 2,511 wheat and cattle farmers folded. An additional 1,807 are expected to quit, leaving 26,700 farms in the state, according to the North Dakota Farm Service. Farm income has nose-dived 98 percent in the state—from $764 million in 1996 to $15 million in 1997. The state once had the distinction of having the most millionaires, per capita, in the nation. In the 1970s, the farmers/ranchers saw their land triple in value. Cattle and grain prices were good—Eureka, instant wealth.

New homes were built, and farmers bought more land, bought new state-of-the-art machinery, bought computers to keep watch on their investments, sent their children off to college—went deep into debt. The economic recession of the 1980s, followed by a severe drought, then excessive rains, conspired to change this status. Farm foreclosures followed, dozens a day, creating more quiet farms. More than 40,000 farms were lost in a 40-year period (1940–1980) when the number of farms decreased from 75,000 to 33,000. The exodus continues into the 90s.

There are fewer millionaires now. The farm exodus destroyed the towns' infrastructure. Another town disappeared. Presto, instant poverty. Weather and economics are cruel masters.

Some of the most widely recognized differences are in the western half of the state. The rivers flow from west to east, and in the eastern half the rivers flow north or south. In the west, generally pronghorn antelope and rattlesnakes are found. In the East, mule deer, pheasants,

ducks and geese are hunted and vegetation also differs. East River Region is known as the tall grass country, and the West River as short grass country.

The Scandinavian-American residents of the East River country feel they are more sophisticated than those in the west, they drink lots of black coffee, root for the Minnesota Twins and wear seed caps and call themselves farmers if they are involved in agriculture. They view the western side of the state as a "nice place to visit." By contrast, the West River residents see the eastern end as a "place they'd rather not visit." They drink their coffee with lots of cream and sugar, root for the Denver Broncos, wear cowboy hats and call themselves ranchers if they are involved in agriculture. The two halves of the state have never been balanced, from that fact stems many of their differences.

Cattle made the town of Carson in the early part of this century. The place sits smack in the middle of the great grasslands. A local rancher said, "When I go to the big cities like Denver, I can't imagine what all those people, in all the tall buildings, do to earn their feed."

Once the cattle were fattened in the feed lots, they were sorted by weight and brands, checked for ailments and shipped by the Northern Pacific trains to slaughter houses in St. Paul or Chicago. But the market changed and the fattened cattle were moved to Denver or Nebraska by livestock truck haulers. The railroad was no longer used to carry cattle.

When the wind is blowing, the wafted dust carries the mingled pungency of cattle feed and natural fertilizers, and the most popular reading material is a magazine titled "Calf News and Feedlot."

There never was a spectacular boom in Carson, but there were many busts. A few buildings remain, a few of them occupied, but it has more ghosts than people. A handful of residents hang on, each for their own reason, and most will likely die amid ghostly remains of the crumbling buildings. On the vast prairie there are no vistas, no magnificent mountains, no coursing waterways. There is only prairie grass, which appears to be untroddened.

Eastern residents, many of them college educated, have a different perspective on the same issues, than those in the west. The economics are different, it influences their decisions. Cattle ranchers in the west are interested in the cattle prices in Denver; wheat farmers are concerned about the world market, and eastern farmers watch corn and soybean futures. They move their products to the corn and soybean refiners along the Mississippi River.

A man with a chunk of land on the east side of the Missouri is a farmer and in the west he is a rancher. A cow on the east side is milked, and on the other it is herded, punched and branded.

4

The Outback: The Promised Land

THIS IS VERY BIG COUNTRY, where distances are great and agricultural towns with little populations are spread throughout the land. For those interested in traveling through endless miles of a "sea of wheat fields," this country is for you. Lying near the Canadian border, this territory requires a long drive through remote expansive countryside, with only a hint of human population, other than a few settlements and their effects on the landscape.

The Midland Continental Railroad (MC) had a bold plan to connect Winnipeg with the Gulf of Mexico, a distance of 1,800 miles. The promoters reasoned that if there was a need for several east/west transcontinental lines, there was also a need for a north/south transcontinental line. Eleven east/west transcontinentals were built in the U.S. and Canada but no true north/south line. The name was fitting, since it would join the midsection of the nation. It was well-financed, but ill-conceived and 20 years too late. Jamestown would be the continental headquarters. It would be a major rail hub; it would rival Chicago in importance.

The 71-mile line opened for business in 1912. It connected with the SOO LINE at Wimbledon, the NP at Jamestown, and the Milwaukee Road at Edgeley. MC officials were filled with visions of grandeur with the promise of a "Winnipeg to Gulf line." Some 200 people turned out for the celebrations.

The line flourished for a number of years, but it never made money. Operating a cantankerous runt of a railroad was difficult. Because grain hauling was the economic main stay. The Midland was entirely at the mercy of the weather and poor crops, all grown within 30 miles on either side of its meandering rails.

The floods of 1969 destroyed the road bed, and it could not recover. Stations like Johnson, Hurning, Homer, Sydney, Millarton, Nortonville, Franklin and Winal were cut off from all rail service. The last train on the Midland operated on October 29, 1970. The 65-pound rail was pulled up and sold as scrap, the few railroad buildings were crushed. The locomotives and rolling stock were sold or scrapped. Nothing remains of the line. None of the cars were saved for museums. The wind, snow, rain and dust returned the land to prairie. The sad little railroad and the small towns did not have a chance in the turbulent business world.

The little line started nowhere, served nothing of importance and ended nowhere. The MC was 58 years old when it was laid to rest, and eleven village sites were laid to rest with it. Few mourners were at the funeral, no one cared, and few noticed. While the Midland no longer will haul the wheat, its place in the history will be a gentle one, brightened by adventure, enriched by its usefulness. May the wheat find rich soil and grow tall where once the light rails ran.

There are no tombstones or monuments for dead dreams. Let us all be mindful of the wonderful little railroad that tried to make a difference in the development of the state, and the far off whistle

Millarton located off a short gravel road, on a short gravel road. "Is this a town?" we asked. "This is Millarton," answered resident John Brower. Main street in Millarton has an abandoned house or two, and a population of three. Mr. Brower is retired, likes to fish and is proud of his golf course smooth lawn. He proudly pointed to a vacant lot, where, he said, Norma Delores Egstrom, later to achieve fame as singer Peggy Lee, grew up. Her father, Marvin Egstrom, was the last station agent for the Midland Continental Railroad here. The railroad quit in 1970, the town died, too.

that made dreamers of us all. It was the death of a railroad, the death of eleven villages and the death of an American dream. On Highway No. 281 a few miles south of Jamestown, at a rest stop, is a new railroad station, built to commemorate the railroad. It contains historical information and is dedicated to farmer, Ray Schlosser, who took care of the rest area for 25 years.

Nortonville is off the highway, on a short gravel road, off a short gravel road. A resident said there were 49 people in the town, but we could not tell where they lived. There weren't that many houses. It just meets the qualifications of a ghost town. The elevator tried to stay in business, after the Midland quit, but it had to give up the "ghost." The grain is now trucked to a rail point at Edgeley, a few miles south.

Millarton has literally "bit the dust." In its

heyday, when the Midland ran through here, it boasted of a population of 125, then to 60 in the '60s, dropping to two or three in 1997. John Brower lives in one house. He is retired and likes to fish on the Missouri River and the lakes near Jamestown. He takes great pride in his golf course smooth lawn. His eyes twinkled as he pointed out where Norma Delores Egstrom, later to achieve national fame as singer Peggy Lee, grew up. The house is gone; the lot is vacant. Her father, Marvin Egstrom was the last station agent for the Midland in this town. Memories are precious.

Merricourt was established west of Oakes, when the SOO LINE extended its track west in 1891. It was a terminal, and train crews would work out of here. Locomotives would be serviced here. The early residents expected the rails to end their westward march, stymied by the nonpro-

Ye' old bank building in Merricourt. It has closed and you now have to fight your way in around the trees.

Unusual architecture in Merricourt. The community hall is occasionally used as a family entertainment center and for other social affairs.

A relic of the past in Millarton, and one of the few buildings still standing. There are no functioning establishments in town.

ductive prairie. It began to decline about a year later, when the tracks were extended to Bismarck. They predicted boom times when Merricourt became a terminus, but they reckoned wrong, and today the town consists of a few one-story wooden buildings, a community hall that is still used occasionally, but no other businesses remain. It has declined in population and by 1997 only four people could be counted.

There are differences between a "town" of four and a farm of four. A town has a name, on a sign post, as you enter, and may rate a spot on a road map. A farm does not rate a signpost and you cannot get directions to a farm by a road map. The buildings on a farm are usually well maintained, a ghost town has weathered abandoned buildings. A farmer may drive miles to see a neighbor. There may be a neighbor or two in a town of four. A school bus picks up the children on the farm and in the small town. Both have rural mail boxes. Farm families and ghost town residents go to a larger town for groceries and supplies. In this town there are no tourist facilities, no restaurant, no gasoline station, no souvenir stand, no overnight accommodations. Admission is free at the community hall. All businesses have closed, even the grain elevator. The tracks still go through town but the trains do not stop.

Merricourt is less than five miles from the Whitestone Battlefield State Park, the site of a battle between General Alfred Sully and the Yanktonia Sioux, later called Yankton Sioux, in an 1863 Indian campaign.

Spiritwood has lost its spirit. Some 30 people populate the gravel streets, a garage, a post office and little else. A huge malting plant on the edge of town did little good—most of the workers live in Jamestown, a few miles west.

Sterling, east of Bismarck, began as a NP siding in 1873. First called Sixteenth Siding, then Ballville, then changed to Sterling in 1882, the town is but a shell. It was anemic and near death

Merricourt is growing downward from a population of three. This is main street. There are no tourist facilities; no tour buses stop here. No one is stopping or shopping in the store, which has closed permanently. The Lariat Bar has roped its last customer. Its sales are "off" by 100 percent.

in its infancy, but has survived. The Burlington Northern Santa Fe Railroad (BNSF) (ex NP) main line continues to roll on while Sterling continues to run down.

The glacial drift prairie is a mid-state, north-south range of drainage hills. It divides the state as well as its people. The drift follows the beam where the fertile eastern half greets the great prairie. The transition resembles that between floor and baseboard. Located in the center of the state, the drift prairie slopes gently in a southeastward direction from the north, the tablelands rise in elevation like a staircase. It gradually and gracefully rises by swell after swell without tree or bush, and everywhere there is green grass.

The grasslands move gradually westward and crumble. We saw hundreds of abandoned farms and dozens of ghost towns, but there is wheat in the hills.

Cowboys, rodeos and ranches are the lifestyle in the west, and every visitor to this country is a tinhorn dude. Motels are scarce as are cafes and gasoline stations. The thunder and lightening storms are violent with the everpresent wind. The people are ever watchful for tornadoes in the spring and summer. Travelers don't diddle and dawdle because they have their mileage quotas and the distances are great in this lonely land. Weather can be bad. Spring, summer, and fall are telescoped into six months and the wind never stops, then folds into six months of snow drifts and temperatures plunge to the bottom of the thermometer.

High rolling plains of vast proportions constitute the area west of the Missouri River. Population density is particularly sparse with just about every town along the route showing the remnants of a once more populous past, when ranching and grain farming was a more labor intensive endeavor. Some are mere ghost towns, with Tagus or Lone Tree as prime examples. The North Dakota ethic of land hardened and highly independent Christian people surviving in a harsh and unforgiving environment rings true here.

Sterling, east of Bismarck on the BNSF, (ex Northern Pacific) main line is but a shell of its former self. First called Sixteenth Siding, to mark its location west from Fargo. it was then changed to Ballville, (the high school is still called Ballville), then to Sterling, named after Sterling, Illinois. The trains run through as Sterling runs down.

Welcome to Spiritwood, population 30 and not growing. The town has lost its spirit as well as most of its people and business. A post office, garage and a bar remain. Main street shows little activity.

Sterling's main street. Not much to do or see, most everyone left town some time ago.

5

Friendliness and Tranquility

PEOPLE IN NORTH DAKOTA are friendly, probably because they are hardened by the elements and have learned to depend on one another to conduct their livelihood. The population density is so thin, it is said, that if North Dakota's population was spread evenly throughout the state, every person would be out of sight of any other person and very lonely.

Western North Dakota is country where cowboys, cattle, and hay farming are the culture and the only identification you need is a big belt buckle and a big hat. A radio station sends out a weak signal from far away that blares an endless stream of country-western music. North Dakotans listen to more western music than rock 'n roll, but also pay to keep a public radio station broadcasting symphonies.

It is a land of cowboy hats and horse trailers, where men wave at passersby with one finger over the steering wheel. If you want to be friendly and wave at folks along the way, you better know the rules of the game. Waving is a direct way of saying "hello" from a distance. Everyone wants to be recognized. People count here; there are no faceless crowds. Each person is valued as unique.

Indeed, "North Dakota nice" is a much discussed phenomenon in the state. People are honest, incorruptible and slow to insult anyone. If you dial a wrong number, the person on the other end may volunteer to find the right number for you. The people of the state are decent, sensible and nice. They are tough, patient and optimistic, and the talk is about "next year, next year."

Most Dakotans leave their keys in the ignition, but may also have a loaded rifle in the gun rack. An out-of-stater may find this a mixed signal. It isn't. Just don't try to steal the pickup.

The state is full of contrasts and contradiction, within a few minutes you can find someone with an opinion opposite from yours, on any subject. In a few places you can still find a quarter cup of coffee to drink while you argue, then complain about the high prices. The mood of the ranchers and farmers is determined by the events of the day, (weather, farm prices, politics). They hang around the coffee shop like crows on a hitchin' post. The people tend to be conservative, opposing gun control, legalized abortion, environmental laws and looking with suspicion on the welfare cheats and inner-city crime.

They argue about government control, yet find no conflict in farm-support programs. They criticize the help given to cotton and rice growers in the South, yet stand in line to get their annual soil bank support check. They get cheap fuel for their machinery, then complain about the oil companies "ripping them off." They argue about taxes, yet gladly accept free mail delivery and school bus service.

The cowboy stirs two heaps of subsidized sugar into Brazilian coffee, then fumes about squandering tax money. He complains about land-giveaways, yet a good number of them are on the 11 million acres given to early settlers under the Homestead Act. Leaving a dollar on the counter for the coffee, he then complains about the sales tax, growling that it will go to illegal aliens.

He drives his foreign built pickup onto Interstate 94 , financed by a Bolshevik scheme in the mind of Eisenhower, then exits on to a farm-to-market road, another asphalt tentacle in a socialistic twisted mind of spend-crazy governments. He gazes over his wheat and cattle spread, financed by a federally financed loan, then qualifies for an agricultural tax exemption. He does not understand that NAFTA and GATTS allows him to sell his grain to foreign countries. The two-way sucking sound is heard both ways. Wheat and cattle out, and foreign money in, and into his bank account. He leaves the state, on a vacation, from a tax-built and tax-supported airport, or tax-built freeway.

Western ranchers believe strongly in individual rights. They rope and brand their own cattle, carry weapons if they want. A blizzard can kill you. The wilderness is still wild and cannot be analyzed. Though adequately prepared, no Plains resident is entirely safe from blizzards, the excessive winds and snowfall. Today, even with modern equipment, a blizzard causes major disruptions in the area. Evidence of this was heard across the nation when more than 100 inches of snow fell in the winter of 1996–1997, resulting in massive flooding of the Red River Valley.

North Dakota people create their own character and are a blend of the Old West bloodlines and values unique to the American West. Their ways are a mixture of nearly mystical times and new, contrasting elements of the past, the present and the future are apparent. North Dakotan's are proud of their famous sons and daughters. Lawrence Welk of Strasburg, Eric Sevaried, famous radio and TV commentator from Velva; Roger Maris, baseball great from Fargo; and Louis L'Amour, western novel writer from Jamestown; Norma Delores Egstrom, later to achieve fame as singer Peggy Lee, from Millarton. There are others equally as famous.

Some have old country mannerisms and religious customs, but practically all have genuine friendliness and openhanded hospitality, rare in the modern age. Numerous communities were settled entirely by colonists who arrived together from a particular country or from a single city in the "old country." They often took up adjoining homesteads, continued to speak their native language and traded in villages settled by members of their own ethnic group. Norwegians who started plowing while Easterners were still referring to the "Great American Desert," were probably the first settlers who were not trappers or fur traders. Irish and Polish settlers were less welcome than Indians in those days.

On a plaque at the Statue of Liberty, Emma Lazarus wrote "give me your huddled masses, the wretched refuge from your teeming shore." The pioneers who came to settle the land were the "huddled masses." They used their brains, their brawn, muscles, and the experiences their civilization taught them, and worked honestly and honorably in the pursuit of the American dream.

They were like each other, strong in mind, body, and determination, and ready to put up with hardship because they believed in themselves and their new country. The pioneers are long gone and the buildings have been boarded up, but among the ruins are the photographs, the memories that form a part of the American Dream. North Dakota is not a state, it is an institution.

Some North Dakotans own computers and word processors and send fax messages instantly. Some have cellular phones and some have no phones at all. Many are on the Net and use it to catch up on news, weather, livestock prices and the grain market. This is the up-to-date connection to the outside world. Mail is not always delivered every day, and some have no mail delivery at all.

I do not know how many read books, the talk is all TV. There are no public libraries for many miles and there are no paperback book racks at the convenience store/bar on the highway. There are no police stations. You can walk down the deserted street without fear of being recognized or seen and no one cares. There are no curfew laws, no traffic lights, few street signs or street lights.

The people are different from the rest of us. They return the grocery cart to the store. They bike with helmets on, they buckle seat belts, they hold the door open for you and don't leave the toilet seat up. They don't blow their horns or give you the California salute when the light turns green. They wait for you to notice. They are nicer than other people. They follow the rules. Volunteerism is a way of life in most communities. It is the way the ambulance and fire trucks run. It is the way swimming pools, libraries and hospitals are built, and the way dozens of annual social events are staged.

They do smoke a lot. We observed many instances of children and teenagers buying cigarettes at gasoline/convenience stores. While the teenage attendant was 'pumpin' gas or waiting on customers, the children could reach over the counter and, with exact change, they had a pack in their pocket. When quizzed about it, the teenage clerk said, "I don't know 'nuttin' about no cigarette law." They do not follow the rest of the nation in cigarette control, preferring instead to maintain their freedom of choice.

The people live on the land and make their living off the land. They are the Mother Earth people. They are real down-to-earth, self-reliant, fiercely independent and self-sufficient. They treasure and guard their independence, their unrestrained freedom to live as they wish on the open plains. Some are laid back. A story is told of a neighbor calling a neighbor woman, saying he and his family were coming to visit. She made coffee, set the table and waited. No one came. She called back. He said, "We are, but I didn't say when." Later, when they came over and she wasn't home, they called, upset. "But you didn't say when," she replied.

They all want better and wider highways and then lament about the disappearing landscape. They drive a hundred miles or more to shop but find no contradiction in grumbling about how much of the scenery is disappearing under concrete. Most have never seen a traffic jam. The direct costs of providing services to ghost towns, (highway, fire and police protection, etc.) will be passed on to future generations. It is an expensive infrastructure built for the car. Every mile of four-lane freeway takes 40 acres off the tax rolls, and that cost is added to the adjoining taxpayers. Few realize that the migration to the cities is to blame and the cause of many economic and social woes. The decline will continue as oil reserves dwindle and people find it more expensive and more difficult to drive to the larger cities to shop. They will simply move there.

People are beginning to make the connection between the zone laws that mandate larger lots, acres of parking, and wide car-friendly streets. They are beginning to realize that there is a connection to spending two hours on the road to go shopping and the dying local communities. Small town business districts are disappearing, partly because they can not compete with corporations doing business on a national scale, and partly because large cities, such as Fargo, Grand Forks, Minot and Bismarck serve ever larger areas.

The 1970s, 80s, 90s, were the breaking point and watershed in the life of rural America. There was a rearrangement of the population. The old empire was finished. Hundreds of towns were collectively thrown out on their own.

The cities in the East demanded farm products. They wanted three square meals a day, sometimes more, and they were in places where all of these food products had to be imported. The two were made for each other: one set of consumers, the other, the producer, were many miles apart, remote and isolated from the rest of the civilized world. When it came to vittles, the fields of the prairie were the storehouse. The farmers were happy to oblige this thirst, as long as it was paid with good coin.

Almost everything the early pioneers knew has changed in the last 100 years, since that day when the first train whistled into town. The two, (North Dakota produce and the eastern consuming markets) are still there, the steel rails still cross the state, connecting the two, but everything else between them has been changed in a profound way.

Today, it is difficult to look at the remaining small towns and imagine what important lifelines they once provided. Today, it is difficult to imagine they are the endangered species, no matter their pedigree or their accomplishments. Many of the buildings and towns are gone, the railroad right-of-way is abandoned, and the highway skirts around the community.

Some have stories connected with them. Many may be no more than local lore, but others may be true. Let us not dismiss them as having out-lived their usefulness. They are part of our history. They are part of us by virtue of their being woven into the fabric of our history.

The locomotive is a great equalizer, it kills little towns and builds up great cities, and in the same way it kills little businesses and builds up great ones. As the railroads withdrew and the highways expanded, the towns were destroyed, helped by the 800 phone number and later the computer. The people could and would order supplies by the 800 number in a city far away, getting a better price for their products and lower prices for the products they buy.

This is a land, part nature and part man made. The small towns grew up and are still tied to the commerce of the big cities. They must sell and buy from far away places. This is the historical nature of commerce, and is still valid.

Few people in the state have ever heard of Haley, Nomad, or Olga, but these communities barely scratched the surface of the silent towns. North Dakota could boast of over 3,000 place-names, most of which no longer exist. Many changed their names once, twice, three and even four times before settling on a name before they died.

Time and the Elements Have Taken their Toll

THEY ARE RELICS OF THE PAST, these gnarled buildings, the weathered wood and rotting structures of the ghost towns and farm buildings. It is hard to imagine that someone once lived in them—a family maybe, or somebody's grandparents, people who mowed the lawn and washed the windows. Like a decomposing corpse, they now smell of rotting wood. Windows are either broken or boarded up. Walls are stripped and seeping moisture. Some still have a roof and floors, but the wind enters without knocking through a gaping hole where a front door used to be. Most of the buildings in the ghost towns are boarded up or gone.

It is awe inspiring to walk around the abandoned buildings, especially at night. You feel like you're summoning up the spirits of all the people who have lived here, worked here and walked through the streets and into the buildings. It can be creepy. You know there is a ghost. Have you ever looked a ghost in the eye? There is nothing there!

Here and there a ruined barn or house sits under flaking coats of fading paint, its roof buckling like the swayback of an old packhorse and the far-off horizon peeking through the empty doors and window frames like a ghost world. It is a peaceful countryside. The real world seems worlds away.

Life seems old here and time goes slowly, and it is so quiet. The past that resonates here was created by hard working god-fearing people from Europe, who produced a bountiful harvest of high-yield, high-protein red durum wheat for the world's bread tables. A bonanza of "North Dakota gold" yielded wealth beyond belief.

Towns that try to reinvent themselves are two for a dime in America. The old towns are unique. Aging has taken its toll, and the changing economy has passed them by. But the vision and tastes of a bygone era remain. They are worth the stop.

Early in the century and into the 1920s, 85 percent of the population worked in agriculture, or lived in rural communities, but by 1995, less than three percent were on farms. The change is not new, but what is new is that it is happening faster than ever before and is happening to the rural population.

What is the price of the escalating changes? It means that communities must turn on a dime to compete. They must work fast. Residents want top notch service, fast action and low prices, except for the things they sell. When the services don't meet the customer's expectation, they go under or face extinction. Communities that stagnate fall behind. For the quintessential small towns that have framed whole lives from birth and marriage to old age and death, the future is far less sure.

It is a little like chasing lost cities. You can't find many of them by reading road maps; you have to do some research to find them. It's a cross between an expedition and an adventure. It is a slow

There is a plaintive wail; ghostly winds echo in the hills. Relentlessly time and weather have conspired to ruin this home. This is a house with nobody in it. The residents fled long ago. It's a house that longs for a family. But only white-clad spirits live here now, making unearthly noises. Or maybe it's just the wind!

If I had some money and my debts were paid,
I'd fix the house and sit in the shade.
The house had a sheltered life,
Putting its wooden arms around man and wife.
It echoes the cheer of a baby's laugh.
No records were kept, not even a photograph.
The spirit of a ghost of a man named Ben
Shares the moment with a boy named Ken.

dismantling in the name of progress and by vandals. North Dakota's farming history gave birth to at least 150 plus ghost towns, 70 of which we visited. Behind the old buildings and scattered bits of rusted tools lurks tales of those early days.

Towns were built over a century ago, almost over night, with the coming of the railroad, to reap a golden harvest of wheat. They died a lingering death when the prospects for riches petered out and the price of farm crops went bust. Today,

many of North Dakota's ghost towns are merely town sites, with nothing more than a pile of bricks and scattered wooden buildings to hint that many people once lived and worked there. Some structures, built almost a century ago, have succumbed to heavy winter snows.

Born during the major town building era early in the century, towns shriveled and began to die during the "dirty thirties," a time when all living creatures suffered from the scorching sun and

Home, home on the range, where seldom is heard an encouraging word, where the house is silent all day. A walk inside these old buildings, stepping over newspapers on the floor, in this old house and farm west of Page, seemingly awaits to be lived in again. The door is unlocked, trusting you will close it after visualizing the era it once served. It is a reminder of the way things used to be. The combination of low prices, hard times and the pressing need to expand forced many farmers to give up their farmsteads and move away. Scenes like this are increasingly evident.

"that incandescent sky fermented them." By the 1920s, the towns began to decline. Some of the faithful in and around the villages cling to a tenuous hope that the places will somehow stir from their comas. The small villages had become less useful in the emerging economic order, socially superfluous and marginal.

Ghost towns, whether privately or publicly owned, seem to be fair game for scavengers. People don't think! Their attitude is: "I'd better take it before some one steals it." Ghost-town hunters will develop their own set of unexpected encounters in the process. The only thing fans should take from the scene are photographs tailored for cherished memories. People did the same with the Roman Coliseum, tearing off its marble for sinks. The only reason there is anything left of it today is because it was too big for them to carry off. Ghost towns are our heritage, our pioneer spirit and people need to preserve their past.

As the hopes, dreams, and fortunes plummeted in the 60s, 70s and 80s, the farms were abandoned and left ruins like this on the prairie. These are the slums of today. The fantasy upon which the farm was built believed in the desire for an ideal "little farm" in the natural landscape, someplace removed, unique, serene, and rural. The farms suffered equally with the towns.

Crops, but no young minds, grow in this abandoned school yard in Cummings. Mother Nature's grass is foreclosing on the property.

In the Backwash

THERE WERE MANY OTHER PLACES that did not rate a place on a road map. LaMars, Oswald, and Norway were only small elevators on a railroad siding. Hove's Mobile Park City and many others in the backwashes were never in the mainstream of the state's history. LaMars, in the southeast corner of the North Dakota, Minnesota, South Dakota triangle, died in 1948 when the township officials refused to allow the sale of beer in the only store. The store, building and all, moved to Hankinson. The population dropped from ten to four to two, then one, leaving just the grain elevator, the manager's house and a township hall. These sites languish in the obscure eddies of state history.

In the southeastern corner, Oswald, population 0, was seven miles west of Fairmount. It was first called Seven Mile Tank and was established by the SOO LINE Railroad in 1890. Fairmount was originally known as DeVillo and changed its name to Fairmount in 1887. Sonora, seven miles west of Fairmount, was a Great Northern water tank originally called Theed. It had a population of 25 in 1906, then it disappeared. Veblen Junction, four miles west of Fairmount, was a switch-off point for the Fairmount & Veblen Railroad (F&V). The F&V, a short-lived line, was taken over by the SOO LINE shortly after it was built. The parallel track was removed, and the name removed from the railroad timetable. These sites were nestled next to a major highway and the main line of the SOO LINE Railroad, but neither did much, if anything, to keep the places alive. Only a handful of people called them home, and today no one does. The Great Depression, drought, and a change in the railroads' operation garroted the life out of them. In such surroundings, these small hamlets were born, lived and died. People there are none. Not even a ghost is around to tell. It made little difference what the places were called, for the little hamlets were doomed to die. What the railroad created, it could destroy, and it did.

Tyler died when the Milwaukee Road (ex Fargo & Southern), pulled up its tracks in the 1970s. While I was taking photographs, a curious resident said, "Not many people come to our town any more." It lies south of Wahpeton, but does not serve as a bedroom community.

Dwight, Barney, Mooreton and Great Bend all have populations below ghost town status. They survive, with no stores, probably a gasoline station, no garage, and maybe a church in town. Some evidence was found where the tracks used to be, but they have been gone a long time.

The early settlers were encouraged to take their chances on life in Dakota land. The westernizing impulse was strong. This was bonanza country. They came, they tried, they lost. They planted trees, they intended to stay. They came with dreams in their eyes, hope in their hearts, a Bible in their hand and seed grain in their pockets. The land was often inhospitable, commerce was nonexistent, settlements few and far apart

Main street, LaMars, all of it. One house, one elevator, one man, one dog and one mail box identifies it as a community. It is not shown on road maps, and was found by following the SOO LINE railroad timetable. It lies south of Hankinson, and just about touches the South Dakota border.

and weather wickedly unpredictable. There is not much shade in the summer nor is there much shelter in the winter. There is not much to stop the winds, and the prairie offered nothing to soothe the senses, and the bent grasses hint of the power of the unseen winds.

The early white pioneers perceived these lands as a wilderness, a land of darkness, which had to be overcome, subdued and conquered by the brave European settlers. The land had to be tamed by farmers and ranchers, who had to convert the wild land into a better use.

In the path of these pioneers lay not only wild lands, but wild savages who also had to be conquered for the benefit of progress. As they traveled in the prairie, they found themselves, at last, on the far brink of civilization. In front of them were opportunities and adventure.

The state was in the far north, its winter too cold, its summers too hot, to attract normal Yan-

kees as they moved west from the east coast in the 19th century. Instead the Scandinavians, the Germans, the Finns, and Russians settled the flat lands, and they brought with them strong social values. North Dakotan's are proud of their ethnic heritage.

The rains came to the land too seldom, the grasshoppers came too often. The winds were often so strong that most of the scenery was in the air. They were born with dust in their veins, baptized by economic fires, and died in an era of nondevelopment.

In the bare-knuckle towns of the booms and busts, the pioneers came with their sweat and dreams, but they met failure. They faced a frontier as fresh as the newly plowed sod, and through it all surged the economy. On the prairie, human life always seems to be working upstream, fighting climate, economics, isolation, law, politics, distance, injustice, heat and cold, and the con-

LaMars, population one, lies close to the South Dakota/Minnesota border. This is country for corn and soybeans, grown in the rich Bois du Sioux River Valley (headwaters of the Red River). A SOO LINE train (now Canadian Pacific), collects a few grain cars on the former Fairmount & Veblen branch (F&V) in mid-July 1995. The SOO's track parallels the region's population in many ways. The small settlement could not survive without the tracks. Both the railroad and the people are hard working, devoted to their labors and dependable. This 1995 scene tells a story, repeated many times over the rail lines of the state. A derailment near this elevator a short time ago, closed the line. Local farmers gathered with caterpillar tractors, semitrailers, and heavy equipment to put the cars back on track. Neighbor helping neighbor. The SOO is just one of the folks.

flicting demands of competition. For most towns it was "uphill in all directions."

As a region, it is transitional because it represents space, freedom and individuality, and conquest. The towns were dwarfed by the vastness of the sweeping landscape.

These are the sights and sounds of the backwash communities, its withering communities, and its people. On the prairie, and elsewhere in the Midwest, hundreds of towns are in danger of being totally abandoned. In the postwar boom, we Americans happily allowed our towns to be dismantled and destroyed. We were so enchanted that we could save a "bundle" by shopping in the

big box stores, that we did not notice that we were throwing away millions in the destruction of our civic life.

Many towns became a dispirited collection of eviscerated homes and vacant lots. Aging business buildings are open to the sky. Grass rises through the gravel street, a dog can cross without looking. Motorists coast through stop signs—there is nothing to hit on the other side. Empty lots, like gaps between teeth in a rueful smile, sprout weeds where houses used to be. Once busy railroad tracks are unused. Perhaps the futurists are correct and the rural landscape of our time will be razed and sown with wheat.

A County Seat in a Ghost Town

MANNING AND AMIDON are on the Missouri Slope, the general eastward slope of the terrain in the southwest part of the state. Manning, county seat of Dunn County, boasted a population of 300 in 1920, and the last reported figure was 42 in 1980. Amidon was the projected terminal for a Milwaukee Railroad branch line extending from New England. The line was never extended, falling 20 miles short of the intended destination. From a population peak of 162 in 1930, it had slipped to 24 in 1990. They are both quiet towns. Their best attraction is that they are remote and their worst attraction is that they are remote. There are no bus-line tours, no hotels, no fast food chains, no gift shops, and no lines of Winnebagos.

Amidon was a void on my road map, a suggestion that only emptiness awaited me, and that is what drew me to this place, which by some definitions, is the most remote town in the state. It is far from a railroad and an Interstate highway. This is the highest county seat in the state, at 2,800 feet. The highest peak, White Butte, 3,506 feet, is only a few miles away.

Amidon was a stage and freight wagon stop on the Medora/Deadwood route. Businessmen, teachers, miners, mule skinners, fortune hunters and women of questionable character rode the stages, after riding NP trains to Medora. Amidon may qualify as a ghost town by the criteria set by the U.S. Census Bureau, but it is the liveliest of ghost towns. The county has a stable tax base and is able to support the county expenses. There are no traffic lights in the county and few stop signs,

and the cattle grazing along the roads, far outnumber the cars and people.

Slope County, of which Amidon is the county seat, is ranch country. It has 1,226 square miles of grazing land, and boasts a population of 900 people, less than one person per square mile, probably the least populated county in the nation. Slope County once had 43 recognized "sites." Today only two remain: Amidon and Marmarth. The latter has a population of 190. Ahead is a dubious tomorrow and they may disappear as have 41 other sites in the county.

Most of the 24 people in the town work at the courthouse, save for a couple of people who run the "store" (bar) and the school bus driver. The 20 children from the town and nearby ranches are bused to Bowman, every day. These children will travel 100,000 miles, or more, on a bus before they graduate. The town boasts of a full-time sheriff, Pat Lorge, who said "Nothing ever happens in this county." A new fire station and a new Lutheran Church are in two square blocks.

Manning and Amidon compete for the title of the smallest county seat in the nation. Both were selected as county seats during the settlement years after the turn of the century, when a county seat meant security. Lack of growth, lack of a railroad, and thus the lack of any meaningful industry and dwindling population forced the towns to downsize, but the county government remains, though no one knows for how long. From a peak population of more than 300 in the '20s, they now report a population figure of below ghost town status.

Amidon, population 24, of which 21 work at the Slope County Courthouse. The business district of the town consists of a church, a bar/gasoline/ convenience store and a few houses. This scene in 1997 shows the "busy' main street.

There was a deep-felt need for this church in Amidon at one time. Country churches dot the country side, their spires rising above the prairie. As many as 300 country churches are still active, though many have closed, as has this Catholic church in Amidon.

The Slope County Court House in Amidon is the most impressive building in town. It is the nerve center for 900 people in the county and 1,286 square miles of cattle grazing lands.

Trains Don't Stop There Anymore

ST. ANTHONY LIES, or, it might be better said, hangs between Mandan and Flasher on the grassy prairie. This is cattle country. It once had a railroad, a 30-mile NP branch line from Mandan, built in 1966 as a short cut to the Mott line. In 1966, some 70 miles of the Mandan/Cannonball/Mott line was abandoned when the waters of Lake Oahe flooded the west bank of the Missouri River. The 30 or so people in St. Anthony are held together by the Roman Catholic Church and school. Weekly freight trains did not haul much; the cattle went to packing plants in South Dakota, (Sioux Falls) Nebraska or Denver, and the small amount of wheat, left after feeding the cattle, could easily be trucked to rail heads south or north. The line lasted until 1986. The Mott line had served its purpose and was no longer needed.

Four stations (sidings) were built along the new cutoff line: Lynwood, St. Anthony, Inverlac and Fallon. They were built to serve the cattle shipping industry, but the business never developed. The markets for grain and cattle went in the opposite direction. The Mandan/Flasher cutoff line was built too late. No industrial development occurred, the markets had been established long ago. The small towns could not catch up.

Fallon became a stage stop in 1877, on the Mandan/Flasher line. The stage service was later extended to the Black Hills. However, competition from rival Medora/Deadwood stage line forced the line out of business and put the town

out of business as well. It became an NP side track in 1966, but it became a true ghost town in 1986, when the tracks were pulled up. A post office was established in 1900, then closed in 1914. About ten people have lived here, at one time, since its founding in 1890. It never attracted any real development.

Flasher was on the Northwest Express Transportation Co.'s stage line, a 240-mile route from Mandan to Deadwood, starting in 1877. Twenty-one way stations were established—two were overnight stops—using 26 concord stages and 200 teams, carrying about 68 passengers per day. One way fare was $23, about ten cents a mile. A shorter stage route from Pierre to Deadwood by the same company forced the Mandan/Deadwood stage line to cut back to three per week. It discontinued in 1890.

Drive slowly, ghost crossing. Burt and Carson are little towns with no water tower, only a few houses in each, and always an abandoned grain elevator. They have a tired look. In fact, they might be the weariest, most worn-out towns in the state. It was as if we were looking at prehistoric ruins that had lost their pep and vinegar long ago. We felt the lonely silence. It was hard to believe that for 75 years these towns hummed with square dancers and laughing children playing excitedly in the cool of the evening. A strange feeling of sadness came over me. We were saddened by the number of abandoned grain elevators (every ham-

Burt is airy, scary, dusty and deserted. Baled hay lines main street. Spawned as a Northern Pacific trading center in 1910, the settlement was home to only a handful of people. Only a few determined inhabitants were shuffling around, like lost souls, when the last census was taken. Strangely absent are historical site roadside markers to describe the role the NP played in the history of the region.

Repair business is slow in this garage in Burt. The mechanics have taken a long, long lunch break.

A reminder of more prosperous times in Burt. No commercial businesses are open here. This was the general store. The old building dates to settlement days, and remains standing. Remains of other business establishments are hard to locate here.

Where Lives the Spirit
An old store on the road to decay,
Ghosts a plenty are around to play.
We'd fix it up like it used to be,
Then give it to people for free,
And make it into a business once more,
Now it is lonely, empty and sore.

let had one or two) and spooky buildings. When the railroad quit, the elevators quit too, as well as most of the business. A cemetery remains.

On a line west of Lemmon, South Dakota, on the Milwaukee Railroad in southwest North Dakota, are ghosts of Petrel, Haynes, Bucyrus, Gascoyne, Scranton, Buffalo Springs, Griffin, Rhame, and Ives, sort of a ghost town trail. The buffalo no longer roam on the home on the range, and the towns seem to be going the way of the once mighty bison—near extinction. The buffalo and fur traders are gone, and the towns, depots and branch line tracks followed them into oblivion.

Even with the advantages of a main line railroad and U.S. Highway No. 12, they lost out to other towns in the survival game. The ghost trail starts at Thunder Hawk, where U.S. Highway 12

and the Milwaukee Railroad crossed into North Dakota, near Hettinger. To modern travelers, speeding past, these hamlets much resemble one another, yet their largely unrecorded histories are as vivid as any in the archives.

On an obscure branch of the Milwaukee Road (now abandoned) in southwest North Dakota are the ghosts of Selfridge (in the Standing Rock Indian Reservation), Shields, Freda, Raleigh (first called DogTooth), Brisbane, Leith, Elgin, Bentley, Watrous, Regent and Havelock. In this string of ghosts, Leith is the metropolis. It just meets the requirements of a ghost town, boasting a population of 50, so is at the top of the cutoff point for inclusion as a ghost town. The line was closed with the bankruptcy of the transcontinental Milwaukee Road in 1977. The route ran through non-

South of Mandan, along the Flasher cutoff line that parallels state highways No. 6 and 21 and then west to Mott, the right of way can still be seen although much of it has been overgrown with grass or plowed under by nearby farmers. The Mott line ran straight west from the Missouri River, then stopped when the farm land ended and the grasses began, or when the construction money ran out. Passengers rode this line until the 1950s, and freight service continued into the l980s.

To the demolition-minded NP, later the BN, there was nothing to preserve. There are no monuments or roadside markers to mark the spots, such as those to locate the early stage routes. The owners, the BN, gave up on the branch line and walked away. The rails were lifted and sold for scrap to make automobiles or razor blades.

What's left are remnants of an agricultural-based economy in tiny Burt. We were appalled at the number of abandoned grain elevators, there were dozens, if not hundreds, scattered along the abandoned rail lines. Every ghost town had one or more. The twin elevators at Burt are like giant tombstones standing in a graveyard of ghost towns.

productive territory, serving only small towns and virtually no industry. The rail line and the towns could not survive. Left behind are ghost towns with names both hopeful and derivative of the pioneers and cultural mix.

This is an example of how a town was born and died, almost overnight. Leff sprang up quickly, the way you would expect it to spring up. It was founded in 1907 along a line supposedly in the path of the coming Milwaukee Railroad. It had a saloon, a hotel, a restaurant, and a twice-weekly, six-horse, sixty-mile stage line to Dickinson. It was ready for the railroad. The railroad came through later in 1907, but they planted a boxcar for a de-

pot one mile west, built a side track, called it Reeder, and invited Leff to come to them. They waited, and the people came and the Leff businesses came too. The town site battles were never equal. Local people had little choice in townsite selections; the railroad always won. They had the track and the outlet to the world. Reeder was built to follow the track, east and west, then later, as it grew, it built at right angles to the track. Today, Reeder survives because of the railroad. Although small in population, it has earned its place as a grain gathering point. Leff lasted only a year or two, but 60 years later Reeder is still on the map. This is the way one town survives while another dies.

For a time Carson was a cattle and grain gathering point on the Northern Pacific's Mott line, but that activity ceased. The world essentially passed by the settlement, which is now a community nestled in the land of "used to be."

Blind ambition and expansionist's plans led to the downfall of these communities. The completion of rail lines only ten to twenty miles apart that essentially competed with each other for limited business was a costly war and the making of a financial disaster. When the war ended, there were 150 or more "graveyards." No one was around to save them from total annihilation. They lost the battle before they even got into the game.

A few towns in the southwestern corner had their start as way stations for stage lines. A stage line was established to connect Fort Abraham Lincoln at Bismarck to Fort Keogh, near present day Miles City, Montana, in 1867. Ten way stations were established along the mail route, a 290-mile run, of which 170 miles were in North Dakota. The route strayed away from the badlands—its operators said the land was too rugged for safe operations, and angled south. Fourth Station, eight miles northeast of Hebron, did not have a formal name. The operators chose instead to use numbers. Moltke was between the fourth and fifth stations, six miles west of Hebron. After abandonment, the residents moved to nearby Hebron. Young Man's Butte, two miles south of present day Richardton, was the fifth way station west of Bismarck. It had a barn, spare horses, a corral, living quarters, and 50 to 60 cabins. It was later used as a construction camp for the NP, but lost its importance when the railroad was completed and was abandoned in 1882.

Green River became the sixth station, one mile northwest of present-day Gladstone on the east bank of the Green River. Antelope way station, eight miles south east of Dickinson, was the seventh station. Double Wall station, eight miles south of Belfield, served as the eighth station. Sand Creek, six miles north of Amidon, became the ninth station, followed by Little Missouri station, the tenth station, about 12 miles northwest of Amidon. Way stations were established about 15 miles apart. The early stage coach/freight wagon routes were little more than muddy dusty trails. The "town" sites were marked off, but most of them had questionable titles. These were the trails blazed by Native Americans, Lewis and Clark, fur traders, prospectors, cowboys, and railroad builders.

It was a labor intensive and costly enterprise. Roads (trails) were carved out of the wild lands, (no tax built roads then). Roads were mostly made of dirt. They suffered badly in inclement weather and were inestimably slow. There were no motor vehicles needing an improved road. The internal combustion engine was far in the future.

Way stations were built, passengers and freight

St. Anthony survives under the influence of the Roman Catholic Church and school.

St. Anthony once had a railroad, a 30-mile Northern Pacific branch from Mandan. The railroad lasted 20 years. No business was generated and there was no hope of any. The main street supports a few businesses and 30 people today. It is difficult to understand why the public would destroy its lifeline to the world, a line that connected one community with another. There are no railroad historical markers, only a strict "no hunting" sign along a farmer's boundary line.

The post office in St. Anthony. The state is dotted with 484 post offices, many like this. Some have full-time postmasters, others are open half days, using a contract employee. The front porch of this house serves as a mail distribution point for the local ranchers, and is open only in the morning.

wagons were protected by a shotgun rider (no state troopers then). Way stations were supplied with food, feed and care for humans and beasts, at a high cost. They were of the "6-8-10" variety: six miles an hour, eight passengers, ten cents a mile. Freight costs were $1 a ton per mile, and a wagon carried about three tons, at four to five miles an hour. Stage/wagon drivers and "shotgun riders" drew about $100 a month for a 10- to 12-hour day. It was bone-crushing work. The NP changed that ratio dramatically to "30-30-3," thirty pas- sengers, thirty miles an hour and three cents a mile. Freight costs were reduced by two-thirds and speed increased to 30 miles an hour, while carrying 30 tons. Stagecoach lines were abandoned after 1882 when the NP was completed. That was the way a stage and freight wagon line died.

Following the building of the highways—first a gravel road, later a hard top surface—some way stations were converted to auto way stations of- fering gasoline, repairs and food. Today most of those have disappeared.

Places to Remember

ON A 127-MILE BRANCH of the NP, south of Mandan, sits the underwater graves of Schmidt, Huff, Fort Rice, Cannonball, and Solen. The line was locally known as the Cannonball branch. Nineteenth Siding was built in 1890 to note that it was 19 miles south of Mandan, and later was renamed Huff. Seventy miles of the Cannonball line was abandoned in 1966, when the waters of the Oahe Dam flooded the line and the towns. Loyalty was strong in these towns but it was not enough to save the towns from the waters. The railroad was not unhappy about abandoning this line because of unstable ground at milepost four near the Heart River, and dwindling traffic volumes.

The Cannonball line was originally part of an ambitious plan to build a line from Mandan to Galveston, Texas, 1,800 miles away. A town was established on the South Dakota border and it was named Nosodak to note its location. This ambitious plan died in 1914, but the town lasted about 30 years as a construction camp, though nothing was ever constructed. The town remained a ghost town and was finally buried under the flood waters of Lake Oahe.

The NP changed its mind about the extension, turned its attention west, and completed a 91-mile extension to Mott in 1910. There was also a plan to extend the line to central Montana as a bypass around the badlands. The 206-mile section between Mandan and Glendive, Montana, was

an operational headache because of the undulating terrain. The line was never built beyond Mott.

Had the NP fulfilled its plan to build to Texas, had the Edgeley/Cannonball line been extended to connect with the Mott line, and had the Mott line been extended to central Montana to bypass the badlands, the face of North Dakota would have dramatically changed. Cannonball would have been the hub for two transcontinental lines. We can only speculate on "what might have been." The Mott line extension added 13 more stock loading and grain gathering locations in an area that had needed a railroad for 20 years.

Burgess, Lark, Carson, Heil, and Burt were established between Cannonball and Mott in 1910. They were laid out by the NP with faith and hope. The line was built with used rail from the main line. Burt was first named Thirty Mile Siding to note that it was 30 miles south of the NP main line. Although this portion of the line was not under water, it was abandoned in 1966 as well. The towns could just as well have been under water with those on the line between Mandan and Cannonball.

The Corps of Engineers initiated a project to relocate the NP's 70-mile Mandan/Cannonball/Flasher line in September 1965. The line would be in an impounded area of the waters of the Oahe Dam reservoir. The line was taken out of service and abandoned in early 1967. Beginning

42

The steep hills on each side of the Little Missouri River basin were a helper grade in the days of steam locomotion, and the conversion to diesel electric engines did not change the need for helpers. As long as there are trains making the journey from Medora to Fryburg, as they have for the 124 years since the railroad was built, there will be helper locomotives. This is what defines the railroad in the badlands. The builders chose to build through the badlands rather than around them, providing a causeway for commerce.

On July 9, 1997, a 4,000-horsepower state-of-the-art brute provided the muscle to push an eastbound train up the steep grade. The BNSF continues to match the grade with giant locomotives, and the fight for the summit is about equal. This powerhouse is on the siding at Fryburg, waiting for track authority to return to Medora, 13 miles west. The badlands humbled man, machine and beast.

in September, 1965, two construction crews began building the right of way between Fort Abraham Lincoln, south of Mandan, to Flasher, working from each end. The two crews met at Fallon. The $10 million, 30-mile line was completed in December 1966, and was turned over to the NP. The newly built Mandan/Flasher line was not welcome. No one was at the "last spike" ceremony in Fallon—only a small mention was made in a Mandan newspaper. It was a railroad no one wanted any more. It was a railroad without a purpose. The future of the abandoned towns was bleak when railroad taxes no longer supported them. The towns had committed suicide by letting the railroad quit.

The end of the line was Mott, but it was also the end of the line for the towns in between. The last train rolled out of Mott in 1986, and development came to a virtual halt. There were too many small towns (ghosts) on the 127-mile Mott Line, the trains will no longer "spook the ghosts."

Winona, south of Bismarck, on the east bank of the Missouri River, was a thriving river town in the 1870s, catering to the soldiers from the across the river military camp at Fort Yates. This notorious town, known as "The Devils Colony," had an 1890 population of 150, with a newspaper, hotel and at least nine saloons, and other attractions operating outside the law. The town died in 1939 and is buried under the waters of Lake Oahe, as were other towns of the Cannonball line.

Many names meant a fort and a fort meant many things in North Dakota history. A "fort" is a permanent installation, a "cantonment" meant a temporary place, a "post" was a temporary installation to protect certain things such as a railroad or telegraph office or a stage line. A "camp" was a semipermanent fort, usually used as an overnight stop. North Dakota, had, at one time or another, 26 forts, one cantonment, 43 camps and three

Sully Springs Primitive State Park. Rising 600 feet above the floor, the badlands were bad for stage and wagon routes. General Alfred Sully found water here in 1864, while chasing the Sioux in the Little Missouri basin to what is now Medora, a few miles west. The town has disappeared; only a signpost on the railroad marks the spot. The grass has reclaimed its own. Sully's presence can be felt, and the cry of the Sioux can be heard if you listen to the wind.

posts. The most famous were Fort Rice, south of Bismarck; Fort Abraham Lincoln, south of Mandan, from which Custer sallied forth on his ill-fated rendezvous with Sitting Bull at the Little Big Horn River in Montana; and Fort Buford, near Williston. Most were on the Missouri River and were served by river boats from Sioux City and St. Louis. Later, railroads were built and put the river boats out of business. Then highways were built and eliminated the trains. Then the flood waters of Lake Oahe and Lake Sakakawea eliminated most everything. All military forts and posts were abandoned by 1895; the Great Sioux problem had been solved. The land could now be settled, and Scandinavian farmers replaced the hostile Sioux. So complete was the abandonment and destruction of the forts that in a few years little evidence could be found that most forts had ever existed. The military has been gone for more than 100 years, since before statehood, but the memories and ghosts are very much alive. A sense of the presence of the "Indian campaign" is felt along the river. Fort Buford is preserved as a historical site.

What these towns on the Cannonball line had all hoped for came to naught. They died. The country is considerably emptier today than it was at the turn of the century. The resulting economic woes began the exodus to the larger communities and each "recession" increased the flow. When the economic burden became too great they left for good. Such ripples touch everyone in the rural community. The story of the prairie towns echoes the land itself. The towns that nourished America did not survive to reap the benefits of their hard labor.

These towns were the guardians of the prairie, a guardian we all took for granted but which did not stand the test of time. We never thought it would happen, but it did. We all watched helplessly as guardian after guardian was pulled down. Changes are good but it is hard to swallow when it hits close to home.

Towns did not spring up casually in the West. They were schemed, surveyed, plotted, promoted, and advertised. Lots were sold, buildings built; then they boomed or died. They bought lumber for their buildings and farm implements for the farms. They prospered as farm products moved to market on the newly built railroad. To be left without a railroad was to be consigned to oblivion. It could mean profits for some, financial ruin for others. A story is told of a question posed by a stranger in a boom town: "How could the small town support four newspapers?" He was told, "The town does not support the papers, it takes four newspapers to keep up with this town."

11

Trip Back in Time

MEDORA, A TOWN, WAS BORN. Here was Marquis de More, a French millionaire, who had dreams of the highest order, magnificent dreams, tempered by the grip of reality. Ten million dollars was poured into a cattle-raising and beef-packing scheme. Here, too, was a wheezing young Theodore Roosevelt, who arrived only two days after the completion of the NP on September 7, 1883, and entered into the cattle business. The Badlands would make him a man. These two and others were here to challenge the prairie.

Medora was on the map; it could not fail. It had too many things going for it. It was on a transcontinental railroad, a jump off point for passengers and the shortest route for freight and passengers to the gold fields. The town even had a Western flavor, with an occasional shoot-out in the bar or on the street. Soon Medora had a bank, a church, school, post office, a depot and a newspaper. And de More started and operated (in 1877) a Medora/Deadwood stage line to the gold fields of the Black Hills for the mail and passengers who had no other means of travel, except by walking. Access was by a narrow trail carved out of the prairie grass. Lumber was hauled from the forests of the Black Hills to build 15 way stations, each with a house, barn, and corral. Five had eating accommodations. He stabled 150 horses to pull four stage coaches, each carrying six passengers, eight if you wanted to be squeezed. In good

weather, the 215-mile trip took 40 to 45 hours travel time, with an overnight stay en route, and cost ten cents a mile.

Supply wagons came from the NP's rail head at Medora; each wagon carried 4,000 to 6,000 pounds of bacon, coffee, tobacco, firearms, gunpowder, and lead. Pack horses and mules followed behind with miner's shovels and picks. At rendezvous stations, where supply wagons and stage coaches changed horses and drivers, the noisy animals and the excitement of children and dust stirred up by the wagons added to the frontier flavor. The stages were exposed to Indians and highway bandits. There were no military posts on this route. The bandits wanted the gold coming back from the Black Hills. After a day or two of a jolting trip, passengers had only a bath, a good meal, and a good night's sleep on their minds, and wanted nothing to do with a stage coach—at least not for a while. But usually for those who experienced and endured the trip, the hardship was erased by the excitement of "getting there."

Penel station, five miles south of Medora, and Hanley station, 14 miles south of Medora, were built for the stage line, followed by Concord, so named to commemorate the style of the stage coaches used on the line. Amidon was an important station, which featured all the services needed for the comfort of the passengers. Bowman was the principal way station, and is today a thriving city of 2,071, and seat of Bowman County. Victor and Ash, south of Bowman, disappeared from the scene when the stage line quit. Rainy Butte was established as a way station 21 miles southeast of Amidon. Ladd, on today's U.S. Highway 85, was the last way station in North Dakota before the line slipped into South Dakota, where a station was built in Ludlow. All are gone now. They were ghost towns before there were ghost towns.

The service ended in 1885 after a shorter (170-mile) Pierre/Deadwood stage line began. Passengers and freight came up the Missouri River to the Fort Pierre landing. Later, a railroad was built along this route and pushed the stage/freight wagons out of business. Still later, a modern highway was built and buses forced the passenger trains out of business. Then the airplane pushed the bus out of business, followed by the automobile, which killed the airplane. So goes the evolution of transportation.

By the turn of the century, Medora was a quiet town. The great winter storm of 1886–87 killed thousands of cattle, and the great scheme of de More was over. A friend remarked to Roosevelt that Medora was about to blow away, leaving only a fence post and a hole in the ground. "You're lucky to have the hole," the future president replied. It was a rugged town, and yet too fragile to survive. The business scheme made sense, but the marketplace ultimately rejected the vision. The ghost of Teddy Roosevelt haunts the place, a ghost embraced by time. Medora, population 101, survives as a tourist center for the Theodore Roosevelt National Park, named for the president. It is the smallest park in the National Park System and also is the least visited.

Once They Were Pleasant Places to Live

WHAT FOLLOWS IS A PORTRAIT of the prairie landscape, a complex land caught in a painful rebirth somewhere between a turbulent past and a promising future. The people don't know what they have left, but they know what they have lost.

Standing on the southeastern edge of the Great North Dakota Badlands is Sully Creek Primitive State Park, an escarpment of eroded hills thrust upwards to 600 feet. These eroded hills were formed by millions of years of snow, ice and thaws that carved the land into grotesque shapes. The shaping continues today. Sully Springs probably had a few stores, a school, a church, and a train depot because some passenger trains stopped there. They are all gone now. The town was established by the NP before 1890, but development was so minimal that no population figures were ever reported. It is no longer shown on road maps or railroad time tables. Only a signpost on the railroad shows where the town used to be.

East- and west-bound trains frequently need helper locomotives to push trains out of the Little Missouri River bottom at Medora. Powerful locomotives are cut off, on the "fly," at Fryburg and returned "light" to Medora to assist a west-bound to Glendive, Montana. The badlands are about 100 miles long. They force the mighty Burlington Northern Santa Fe (BNSF) trains to a crawl, and bring the powerful locomotives to their knees, just as they did to General Sully as he crawled through the hills with his two- or three-mile wagon train, chasing the Indians.

Sully's expedition through the badlands was no small operation. It entailed a train of 150 wagons, each drawn by six mules or horses, making a herd of 900 animals. The cavalry battalion required 2,000 horses to carry as many troops, and a herd of 300 cattle were driven along with the train. The badlands humble men, machine and beast.

In Surrey, high-speed freight trains rumble through on the main line—none stop. The few people call it a good place to live, and the town survives on trust, honesty and friendship. A local gasoline station may have a "closed" sign in the window but a few select trusted customers have a key. They pump their own gas, get a few items off the shelf, and leave a "due bill" in the box. The honor system works here; it is small-town honesty personified. This town was featured in a national newspaper as well as in a TV program.

Bonetrail in northwestern North Dakota is as bleak as its name. Its bleached bones are obscured in a high-grass area where nature is reclaiming what she wants. The site is deserted, and its tattered remains are absorbed into a nearby farm. No railroad serves it; no highway passes it.

The towns of Lonetree, Tagus, Blaisdell, Palermo, and Wheelock are nearly dead. Epping eyes, with envy, Spring Brook, its sister ghost to the south with its 32 people. Nesson, east of Williston on the north bank of the Missouri River, flourished for a time. Dependent on river traffic, it survived for a few years after the Great Northern arrived, but died in 1918. Mondak, a notorious town straddling the border with Montana, with most of the businesses on the Montana side, especially the saloons, catered to the whiskey demands of border drinkers. North Dakota was dry. Montana was not, and Mondak owed its existence to the different laws concerning alcoholic beverages. It was doomed by prohibition in the 1920s and destroyed by a prairie fire in 1928.

Tagus, incorporated in 1908, reached its peak of 140 in 1940, then declined to 14 by 1970. The last business closed in 1978. Tagus was dead. The town lies west of Minot. Most of the trees have died as have most of the town's folks. No one was around to explain why the town had to die. There are many luckless hamlets whose rotting houses and fat graveyards tell a story no one listens to. It is possible to hear the prairie wind cutting through the grass, a sound now louder than the heartbeat of the town.

Tobacco Gardens, Banks, Expansion, Senescal, Charlson, Sanish, Van Hook and Elbow Woods have all disappeared under the flood waters of the Garrison Dam's Lake Sakakawea in the 1950s. Most residents moved to the government-built town, which was simply named New Town. They could have combined the names of Sanish and Van Hook and named it Vanish.

Omemee once was to be a rail center. The Great Northern (currently Burlington Northern Santa Fe) and SOO LINE Railroads crossed just out of town. The future looked bright, but the opposite was true. It lost business to other towns established along the SOO. The last business closed in 1969. The SOO LINE tracks have been abandoned and removed, and the town was left to die. Only four crumbling buildings were found, and only three people could be counted. It can hardly be called a rail center or the center of anything.

All along the rail lines, the sky line was littered with abandoned elevators and broken buildings. Rosen and Cartwright fit nicely in the ghost town trail. Both of the towns are on the BNSF Railroad, but the huge elevator complexes in nearby towns forced them to close, leaving a shell and a hole in the ground where viable elevators once stood and a community existed.

In the northwestern region lies Larson, a Pygmy of a place of 26. The odds are good that it will soon be gone, along with Lostwood, now but a signpost on the railroad. And no evidence could be found of Lundsvalley, not even a signpost, although it is shown on the railroad timetable. We did find Battleview, Hamlet, Corinth, Appam, Wildrose, and Hanks. They form a landlocked string of death and dying. Hanks is the westernmost of these settlements, and one of the most ghostly. Present population is 11. It was a colorful Western-style cattle town, a portal through which thousands of cattle were herded through to the rail heads at Kenmare and Bowbells.

"Welcome to Zahl" reads a roadside sign, with a "Viking" painted on the sign. Its 17 people support a church, a post office and a grain elevator. This is Norwegian country. There are no stores no school. Only two streets in Zahl; the longest is a north-south gravel main street. Most of the abandoned structures are on the west side.

Appam became a ghost town, not by choice or chance, but by economic woes. The town was established in 1916, upon the arrival of the Great Northern Railroad. It died in 1972, when the post office closed. Population was never more than 100, and today, only wooden markers on vacant lots indicate the sites of "Smokey's Blacksmith shop, Christianson's grocery store, (it had plate glass windows) the Appam Hotel, the Sons of Norway Hall, the two-story Holm's Pool Store on main street, and where Oliver Holms lived. There was a billiard parlor for the male population, a church basement for the women's quilting bees, a hardware store, and a signpost on the railroad where the depot used to be. A single white mail-box on a corner says "Appam Mail." There is little to do here and all day to do it. Few residents in neighboring towns could remember the hotel or even the town. Old timers had long ago moved to other places, and most have died. Ghosts

A relic of the past near Columbus, and a reminder of more prosperous days. It has that tired look, and only ghosts are lodged in this house. Nature is relentlessly reclaiming the yard, always taking back what is hers. Man only borrows it for a while. Bluestem grass has made inroads on the lawn and driveway.

A bird's-eye view of Columbus, a dying town. The elevator closed, the tracks were removed, and half its population moved away. Its future is in doubt.

Ignore for a moment, the appearance and spread of the rural communities, the highway congestion, the speed of an airplane. North Dakotas's cities, towns, villages and hamlets are the creation of the railroad age.

Proof that the trains do not come through here anymore, this elevator, between Crosby and Columbus, on the wheat fields, was on a branch of the SOO LINE. The track was abandoned, as was the elevator. Small 30,000-bushel elevators once dominated the landscape but could not compete with the 300,000-bushel giants. This small elevator is typical of those found off the railroad and off the highway. The row of rotting ties and weeds growing high on the driveway is the only remaining indication that a railroad came through here. The railroad took back its tracks, the elevator closed, taking the nearby town to oblivion with it. Few regions had a network of rail lines as North Dakota. The proliferation led to redundancy and duplication of service, which led to abandonment. This lonely elevator has seen its last harvest.

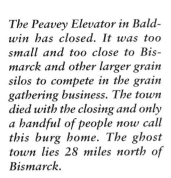

The Peavey Elevator in Baldwin has closed. It was too small and too close to Bismarck and other larger grain silos to compete in the grain gathering business. The town died with the closing and only a handful of people now call this burg home. The ghost town lies 28 miles north of Bismarck.

For relaxation cowboys and ranchers celebrated payday by crowding into the local saloon. When they were sufficiently braced with alcohol, fist fights broke out. There was always a "tough guy" who had to prove that he was the toughest. He usually ended up in the slammer until he sobered up.

The long closed bar and hotel in Palermo has not served a beer-drinking patron nor has any one stayed in the four rooms for many years. It closed more than a half-century ago and now just sits and waits for time and weather to claim it.

A relatively modern school is abandoned in Palermo. It was built with federal money during the Works Progress Administration, later changed to Works Projects Administration (WPA), a Roosevelt administration "New Deal" program in the 30s. The school served the community until the mid 70s. The WPA built mostly brick and mortar structures, as this school house. Some 110,000 public buildings were constructed during the ten year period from 1932 to 1942.

This building in Palermo is for rent or sale, as are many others. The P.C. Paulsen hardware store and garage depicts an almost unrecognizable view from its use many years ago. It is only one step away from the wrecking ball or an arson's match. America is being transformed at warp speed. It is the end for this building and for this town. We look upon anything that is not up-to-date as standing in the way of progress. In our race to build a new society, we systematically undertook to unbuild what had taken generations to create. Palermo appears to be sucked into a vortex leading down-hill to a state of oblivion. This town is following the pattern of a cow's tail: growing downward.

One of the better houses in Palermo; most of the others are abandoned. The barn-like structure fits well with the farm decor. It was built soon after Palermo was founded in 1901. The town was named to honor the capital of Sicily and the many Italians working on the railroad. This house has withstood nearly 100 years of winters and looks as if it could stand another century of service.

are everywhere. During the long silent nights, when the moon is full and coyotes and hoot owls are heard in the far off hills, the isolation is even more real. The four or five people who still "hang" on in this unsheltered land share a yearning for space, a deep dread of congestion and an urge to be unencumbered by just about everything except weather and space.

The towns were peaceful, clean, and secure, but there was nothing much for the young people to do when they finished school. There are few economic structures to build on. They left if they wanted something better. Things move slowly here. The pace of life seems governed by the seasons: slow in the winter, hectic in the summer. The old and new mingle here. Ancient, dilapidated buildings mix with state-of-the-art farm equipment and modern farm houses.

Hobo Kingdom, three miles northeast of Battleview in the northwest corner, was founded by four bachelors. Local settlers bestowed the name to humorously note the cooking habits of the four men. The bachelors and the town site have disappeared.

Wildrose was the end of track on the Grenora Line of the GN from 1911 to 1916, until the line was extended 36 miles to Grenora, where a new end-of-track terminal was established and remains to this day. It was the final blow to Wildrose, and there seems to be little reason to expect the downward population spiral to reverse.

The remains of Ambrose and Alkabo, (the name was chosen to describe the soil, alkali and gumbo) in the northwest corner, a few miles from the Canadian border, sit in a high-grass area where nature is reclaiming her domain. For a number of years Ambrose grew, then became moribund. Population fell from a high of almost 400 in the 1920s to less than 50 in 1994. Alkabo did not do any better, going from more than 100 in the 1920s to 19 in 1976. It became a true ghost in 1994.

Ambrose was created in 1905 when the SOO LINE made this the western terminus; the town lost out when the track was extended west into Montana. The name is Greek for immortal. The "Queen City of Divide County" competed for the county seat, but lost out to Crosby. It reached its

Water is scarce on the prairie. A windmill is essential. One early settler said he had to haul water seven miles, and when asked why he didn't dig a well, replied that "the distance is about the same in either direction." This windmill, standing like a soldier guarding the frontier, its wooden paddles locked permanently against the wind, has not pumped water for more than five decades, since electric power came to the prairie in the 40s. This ancient relic was found on an abandoned farm near Palermo.

"This well was almost 400 feet deep. The water came up cold and fresh. No contaminated or polluted water came from this well," said a nearby farmer. "It drew about 100 gallons an hour. It took a steady wind, of which North Dakota has plenty, to pull a thousand pounds of sucker rod and 400 feet of water to the surface." A governor controlled the speed of the ten-foot wheel to a speed of 35 to 40 revolutions per minute. The cold water from this well served two purposes: to cool the milk and cream, and to water livestock.

The need for water is still there. The cattle who drink it are still there. Now an electric pump does the work.

The fire station/jail is the most imposing building remaining in Palermo. During the depression years the town fathers allowed transients and wanderers to stay here overnight or longer. Later they thought differently, fearful that the disgruntled and disillusioned travelers might set fire or ravage the place in retaliation against the system. They were locked out, forcing them to move on, taking the next freight train out, which was not always easy since most freight trains did not stop. There were three types of wanderers: hobos who would work, tramps who could work, and bums who wouldn't work. In 1995, when this photo was taken, the fire station was still standing tall and proud, the wanderers are long gone.

popularity in the 1920s when 389 people called it home. But it slipped to 58 in 1980, then to 10 or 12 in 1997. The bar, an elevator and the post office are all that remain. There are no stop signs off the side streets; the few cars can whiz through with little danger of colliding with anyone or anything. The vagrant wind whips up "wind devils." A shutter bangs and a weathered door creaks. Only memories remain and they are getting fewer.

Ambrose was on the Outlaw Trail between Montana and Canada at the turn of the century. Hundreds of horses were stolen by border bandits and funneled through Ambrose into Canada for sale to the Assiniboine Indians, to the Chippewa in the Turtle Mountains and the Sioux on the reservations along the Missouri River in North Dakota. Horse stealing and cattle rustling was fair game on the wide open prairie. Jobs were scarce and stealing was more profitable.

Border bandit George Zeglin (alias Bloody Knife), had been arrested in Saco, Montana, in 1908, for stealing five horses, but was released because of lack of evidence. Bloody Knife rode into Ambrose and began to shoot up the town in a drunken rage, injuring the newspaper editor. He was a mean dude. The people were enraged and took up arms. A hail of 50 bullets flew, and one caught Bloody Knife in the head. His drunken ride was over. He was buried in the Williston cemetery, according to the *Williston Optic* of June 4, 1908. Ambrose has been quiet ever since.

At this writing, Niobe is little more than a hamlet with a sign, a siding, and an elevator. Once the depot was a busy place. A roundhouse held engines ready to work two branches, and the junction hummed with activity. Wheat farmers of Scandinavian ancestry were in abundance. All are gone but for a few wheat farmers.

Coulee, north of Minot, nestles quietly in the fertile, broad Des Lacs valley. It died because it

A few buildings remain on another ranch site near Palermo. Cattle raising is not the main economic mainstay of the area, it is now wheat. A few cattle graze among the buildings, but no one was around to care for them.

A ranch house north of Palermo is all that remains of a vast cattle empire. It looks and waits for the ranch to be resurrected and climb out of its coma. No one was home at the time of this visit in 1992. This photo reflects the desolation and isolation of the broad prairie in North Dakota.

was too close to other communities.

Sutton, sitting astride the Fargo/Surrey cutoff line of the Burlington Northern (ex-Great Northern) lost favor in the business communities. It has had its past but not much of a future. The postmistress retired in August 1995, and the post office was closed. The town of 32 had lost another business. Technically, there are no "postmistresses" as all persons, regardless of sex, make an oath to federal postal authorities to be "masters of the post." The town survives, just barely, but no one can tell how or why.

There is little to do in Danzig. The post office was discontinued in 1912, and the town discontinued soon after. Norwegian, about two miles northeast of Danzig, was established to note the nationality of most of the settlers. The town died in 1899.

This is rural life in the bluestem grass prairie land—North Dakota style. Not too many people want to visit today. There seems to be little reason for the small towns to have been established and little rationale for them to survive.

An overview of Palermo. The Great Depression marked the beginning of the end for most small towns. The continued decline in the number of people and the growing number of abandoned buildings made Palermo a ghost town with no active businesses, no school and only a handful of people. Settled by people of Norwegian ancestry, the inhabitants were the kind of people who needed to live on the isolated plains. It is a place of cold, snow, wind, and hot weather, and is nearly devoid of trees.

In the Scandinavian communities the church has always been an integral part of life. The people came from strong Christian beliefs. This church in Palermo is a well-established Lutheran congregation. The author's father is buried in the cemetery behind this church. The Great Depression and drought garroted the life out of Palermo, but this well-maintained Lutheran church, built in the 1920s, survives and is a testament to the faith of the pioneers who built it and to those who support it today.

A signpost marks the spot where the depot used to be. All vestiges of commercial business have disappeared, except the lone grain elevator. The passing track has been removed, and the speed board tells the trains not to slow down. There is little action at the elevator. To the BNSF, Palermo does not exist.

From the first day in 1827, when the first commercial railroad puffed into life in Baltimore, the location of the tracks, the sidings (which usually resulted into a settlement), the station, shaped the landscape and the destiny of America.

A relic of the past. The weathered wood and rotting structure of an abandoned farm house. It is hard to imagine that as many as 12 people lived in this house during the depression years. This author was one of them.

The long-closed mercantile store in Palermo. Remains of other businesses are difficult to locate. At one time this store had many things for sale, but today there are no buyers. The future is not rosy for this building or for this town.

"Tuffy" Christoffersons' store was heralded with the same pioneer frugality that characterized its owner. No signs marked the building, none were needed. Everyone knew who "Tuffy" was and what he sold. Any advertizing would have been pointless.

When the door opened, the bells tinkled, and the musty smell, the ornate cash register, the shelf of Red Wing shoes, and Clabber Girl baking powder met us as we entered. This is where we bought hard candy at Christmas, and firecrackers and cap pistols for the 4th of July celebrations.

Once upon a time, this building was a one room country school, the Redmond District, some ten miles north of Palermo. A team of horses and a wagon or sleigh were kept at the ready to evacuate the ten or 12 children during a snow blizzard, a tornado, or heavy rains. The wagon was used a few times during the depression years. The school was closed when a new school was built, using WPA depression-era labor. It is now a storage shed on a nearby farm.

A relic of the past in Palermo

The Sons of Norway meeting hall in Blaisdell still offers lutefisk and lefse dinners to a sea of Norwegians, while dancing to "chin music" (fiddle) and pumping out "oompah" polkas on the accordion and base violin. Fiddles were tuned and banjo strings tightened; the local residents enjoyed the pickin' and singin' lasting far into the night. There is no evidence that Lawrence Welk ever played in this town, but many talented local musicians entertained the Norwegians for decades.

A ghost town! A settlement abandoned by its inhabitants, a national catastrophe. Tagus, incorporated in 1908, reached its peak population of 140 in 1940, and declined to 14 by 1970. When the last business closed in 1978, Tagus was dead. The town lies west of Minot. Most of the trees have died as have the people. The town is a bonanza of crumbling, decaying, weird foundations. There is no hope for this ghost town. The weathered buildings stand naked. Time and weather have destroyed them. They had served their purpose and are now banned from the active scene. No one was around to tell us why the town died.

It is hard to imagine that someone once lived here: a family maybe, someone's grandparents, people who mowed the grass and washed the windows. Like decomposing corpses, the buildings smell of rotting wood. Windows are broken or boarded up, the walls are stripped and seeping moisture. Some still have a roof and floors, but the wind enters without knocking through gaping holes where doors used to be. The roof is tattered; inside doors cannot be opened or closed.

Gasoline, groceries and cold beer were once dispensed from this store on U.S. Highway No. 2 at Blaisdell. No one has stopped or shopped here for years. On the highway, it is an abandoned building; on the railroad it is a signpost.

The water tower in Blaisdell, a rarity in a ghost town.

Tagus is worth a stop, not only for the abandoned buildings, but to view the relics of a more prosperous past. The railroad line created a line of settlements that became stepping stones from community to community.

Towns, which at one time were rivals, were suddenly redundant. Nowhere was this more evident then in the "beads on a string" along the rail lines. The towns lasted about three decades.

RIGHT: **Not much remains of Lonetree.** *No one lived here. No road sign or railroad signpost marks the spot. No one cared enough to identify the place. We were chasing a yolk-yellow sunset. It was about 9:30 p.m., June 13, 1995, too late to "tour" the town or the countryside. It is an old town in a new era.*

The Peavey elevator in Lonetree no longer loads grain on track side. The loading spout is tucked closely to the side. This village, west of Minot, was named for a single tree. The community is on the main line of the present-day BNSF, but even the mighty railroad could not save the town.

West of Page, this house awaits the destructive forces of time and weather. Houses like this had lots of places to explore. Old magazines and newspapers were scattered on the rotting floor. The home is an example of how the relentless teeth of nature, with small and large bites, gnaw endlessly at the abandoned works of man.

Although it is a recognized place for the grain people, there are no permanent people here. Russell has found its place in the grain gathering business. A silo (mailing tube) elevator dominates the scene. It is located on the SOO LINE's wheat line, across the northern border of the state. The tall elevator makes the small elevators look like salt shakers. The dreams of the promoters were not fulfilled in Russell. The facts are sometimes hard on dreams. Any chance of growth was retarded by the physical limitations of the environment and by the presence of its neighbor. The town lost all population and businesses to Newberg, only two miles north.

Weary, eerie Erie! No service is available in this garage. A few buildings are around, but most are not used. Little is known about Erie, founded in 1882. It lived a quiet life and died quietly in the 1980s and 90s. It was a dream of the pioneers that did not come true.

Erie sits in a region of prime farming land. Two good highways and a railroad should have guaranteed a successful town, but it didn't. The early settlers believed that the free homestead lands would bring the dawn of a prosperous new era. As the farming pattern changed, the town followed the familiar pattern to oblivion. The population has fallen to below ghost town status. Most of the buildings have been abandoned.

No money in the State Bank of Erie, a few miles northwest of Fargo. Settlers came to Erie to take their chances on Dakota land. They came, they tried, they lost. Today, a few structures settle down to a routine of debilitation and vegetation.

A "hidden house" in Sutton. This house is typical of the many deserted houses in this town. The interior is now filled with "trees from heaven." A faded gas pump stands on a deserted corner, its price is stuck at 19.9 cents a gallon. Sitting astride the Fargo/Minot (Surrey cutoff) main line of the BNSF, the town has lost its importance. It has had a past but not much of a future. The post office is probably the busiest place on this hot June 1995 day, but the grain elevator is its chief economic resource.

The main drag of Sutton. A gasoline station and the post office are the only businesses left, save the grain elevator. They are the most precious of the remaining institutions—all others have disappeared. The postmaster retired in August 1995, and the post office was closed. The town lost another citizen and another vital function.

No more will this church greet worshipers. It has been dethroned and de-steepled. The church in Gardner, has seen better days and waits for those days to return. The early church bells rang to call in the congregations, sound the fire alarm, summon children to school, announce funerals and listed election returns. The bell was finally removed, its duty to the community is over. Did Rev. Boston Smith start this church with his chapel car ministry? Or was it Catholic Father Francis Clement Kelley?

BELOW: *Pillsbury is held in place by the BNSF tracks and is kept alive by the elevator, the town's most imposing structure. It is located midway on the Fargo/Minot Surrey cutoff line. From a past population of 260 in 1930, it declined to 46 by 1995. Lucky are those who still have a rail line.*

ABOVE: *Grano was to be a place of importance. It was selected by the SOO LINE to be the grain gathering point in the fertile Des Lacs River Valley. Grano waited for the people to come, and they waited, but it did not grow. This is the heart of the business district, but now only ghosts are lodged in the buildings. You can walk down the deserted streets without fear of being recognized or seen and no one cares. No one came for their mail. Not a phone booth is in sight, no street signs, no street lights, no traffic signals and no curfew laws. In 1995 only two people were here. They run the bar.*

Grano probably had a depot at one time, but in 1995 all that could be found was a railroad siding and a few steel grain bins. Building for building, Grano is one of prairie's best ghost towns. Old wooden buildings slowly weathering away belie the fact that this community once boasted five elevators, a bustling business district and a newspaper, the Grano Tribune, a weekly, from 1905 to 1918. Bleak and desolate are the words to describe this scene. Ruins of the old store feature windows that gap into nothingness. Somewhere in the rolling hills of the Coteau Valley are the wheat fields that spawned the place. It is a shadow of its former self, snuggled in the quiet recesses of the Coteau du Prairie hills. The countryside is representative of the scenery found through northwestern North Dakota. The land has literally remained unchanged from its settlement days, at the turn of the century, when horses and ranches reigned.

It was a mistake to build the village of Greene. It was a SOO LINE townsite but soon faded when other villages were built nearby. The false front store is about used up. This one says "Sorry we are closed." The two remaining buildings on main street are a weather-beaten store and a ramshackle house. Rain and weather make the gray light on false fronts look like skeletons. Many of these ghost towns have little or no population, but a few old buildings remain. Today they serve nothing. The rivalry between the closely spaced towns, broke the back of many small towns. The speed at which the demise came caught even the most loyal citizen off guard.

This aging warrior in Greene is a lookalike to those in other communities. There were no operating businesses in this town on this day in 1995.

No more will children attend this school in Appam, but the spirit of the children lives here. It is old, dark, and lonely.

Little school on the prairie. At one time there were hundreds of one-room schools on the prairie. Better roads, school buses and consolidations closed many. The dying country school is evident in this scene. Its once white clapboard, now graying under the relentless winds, sun, and weather, will not stand many more winters. Eventually the building will be gone. Lightning may strike the tinder-dry bell tower. A tornado may sweep it away, or it may be torn down for its salvage. For now it just waits and waits.

Someone must have had a good sense of humor when they named this place, Lostwood. The prairie is almost devoid of trees. Once a large farming community of 300, the town consisted of a hotel, cafes, a bar or two, a post office, a grain elevator and other businesses to serve the fledging community. About all that marks the spot is a signpost on the railroad—the side track has been removed—a well-kept Lutheran church on the hill, and a deserted school. No trace could be found of other buildings. The windswept remains of the old town were conceived and died in less than three decades, in the early part of the century. The town pulsated from the farm economy before going into eternal sleep. Lundsvalley, a few miles west of Lostwood, was promoted by the Great Northern, but the railroad station was about the only development. The town has disappeared from road maps and railroad timetables, the site is vacant. The highway and railroad cuts through the prairie hills but neither recognize the place.

The community hall in Ambrose has seen its last dance. With only 10 people in town, dancing partners are hard to find. In the early days cowboys held calf-roping contests on vacant lots, and farmers entertained themselves by horse and tractor pulls, and horseshoe games. Women sat on the sidelines tending to children, quilting or just gossiping.

Ambrose could easily have been named Rip Van Winkle—it has been sleeping for many years. Most of what remains of the main business district is on the west side of the gravel road.

Every day is "gasless day" in Ambrose. If I could tell this story in words, I would not have to carry a camera around with me.

It appears this building could have housed three stores. All have closed, and shoppers shop in other towns. Ambrose's brush with notoriety came in 1908, when horse thief George Zeglin, alias Bloody Knife, in a drunken rage, terrorized the town and shot the town's editor. The residents took up arms and 50 bullets ended his crime career. Could the fatal bullets have come from the roof of this building?

The lighting was not right for this photo of the Masonic Hall in Ambrose, but, then few things have been right for Ambrose in many years. No Masons, or anyone else, have met in this hall in ages.

No one was home at the time of our visit, but they left the door open.

An oversized mail box is the Appam post office. Four names were on the door. The building in the rear appears to be the city offices. Note the street light above the door.

The main street of Appam. Social activities are scarce, except to feel the wind blow, watch the grass grow, walk the tracks, count the ties and swat flies.

Business district of Zahl. Early settlers sensed a song in the wind going through town, like a high note of hope.

Historical markers show where people worshipped in Appam, and where stores were located, where people lived, and where children went to school.

Once a family lived here in Zahl. They trimmed the hedge and mowed the grass. There is no action in this tattered house.

A large community hall in which many functions were held in the days past, in Mylo, stands empty and deserted. The old depot is gone. A SOO LINE freight train (now Canadian Pacific) rumbles through town each day. It does not stop. Mylo peaked at 140 in the 1920s dropped to 32 in 1980. By 1990, it was dead.

Egeland is not a ghost town, although there are pockets of ghostly areas in the settlement. The former SOO LINE depot has been removed from the right-of-way, and restored to its original condition. It is now a museum. Townsfolk once gathered at railroad stations like this one to greet the train, whose arrival was the high point of the day.

No two elevators are exactly alike. In some cases the elevators were built in pieces, as "add ons" to serve a particular need. A lot of things have gone wrong in Battleview in its later years. The community lies in an open grass field, next to the BNSF Stanley/Grenora branch, exposed to the elements. This town is part of a line of "ghosts" where the abandoned buildings are waiting to be reclaimed by Mother Nature.

Architect of North Dakota: Jim Hill's Wheat

OFTEN NAMED after railroad officials or important figures, the settlements had personalities. Most of the personalities have been forgotten. Few people outside of railroaders in Fargo and Minot know where Nolan Junction or Surrey are, and fewer still know who Jim Hill was. That is a pity, for his vision, his high ideals and his achievements were considerable in North Dakota. Jim Hill's venture with the Great Northern (GN) was a gamble and a race against time. The GN is planted like a sprouting couch (quack) grass runner, just below the Canadian border.

During the expansion of the GN, Jim Hill influenced the course of the state more than any other man in its history. He laid and operated more track in North Dakota than any other railroad. The Great Northern laid down 2,027 miles of track and gave birth to 275 town sites; the Northern Pacific operated 1,460 miles and sired 175 sites; the SOO LINE built 1,397 miles and created 157 sites; and the Milwaukee Road ran on 534 miles of track and connected 60 sites. Tiny Midland Continental ran on 71 miles of rickety track serving 20 communities, in the center of the state.

Approximately 400 railroad stations were built in the state in as many towns in a span of 40 years (1880 to 1920). Some 5,388 miles of rail lines were built to connect these communities. The mileage is far out of proportion to the population. The depots and other railroad structures were built of wood and were minimal in size, simple in design, and functional in use. They were cheap to build, and cheap to demolish when they were no longer needed. Larger towns, those that showed some signs of economical justification, rated a brick or stone depot. Few towns outgrew the scale of these small depots.

The GN Railway built 17 branch lines, totaling 1,368 miles. The most famous is the group collectively called the "ladder lines," sprouting northward toward the Canadian border along the main line. The Grand Forks/Minot main line is locally called the "turkey track" because of the many branch lines on each side of the line. The Northern Pacific built 13 branch lines, 1,136 miles; SOO LINE had nine branches and 870 miles; Milwaukee Road, four branches with 218 miles; while the Midland Continental RR contributed one branch line stretching 71 miles. More than 3,560 miles, 66 percent of the rail mileage, was in branch lines.

Most of the railroad structures, (depots, engine houses, coaling and water towers and maintenance sheds), are gone, and in many places the right of way over which the tracks ran has been abandoned. Today there are about five operating depots, mostly used by Amtrak. Remaining buildings, of which there are but a handful, are used for railroad offices or maintenance storage buildings. Today, with good highways extending like spider webs in all directions, it is easy to forget how useful the trains were for fast, efficient travel and shipment of goods.

The state has one mile of track for every 100 people, connecting 687 town sites, a bad ratio for a tiny population. A few inland towns (no railroad) are tucked neatly into the landscape, serving as roadside convenience stops and local bars. Most ghost towns had a bar and a church. The bar is usually the last business to close.

That Jim Hill failed to bring order to railroad expansion in North Dakota was unfortunate, for if his plans had been implemented, the railroad network would not have been so extensively overbuilt. The St. Paul, Minneapolis & Manitoba, forerunner of the Great Northern (Jim Hill), and the Northern Pacific had a gentlemen's agreement not to build lines into each other's territory. It was a one-territory, one-railroad agreement; each railroad would build development lines in its own region. The NP broke that agreement by stabbing tracks north from its mainline, mostly into the rich Red River Valley, which caused Jim Hill to expand his lines south deep into NP territory. The proliferation of rail lines and the many small towns they created caused an overabundance of rail lines and too many small towns, far in excess of the need. The railroad war had started. It caused redundancy, duplication, mergers, sale of surplus lines to regional carriers (Red River Valley & Western and Dakota Missouri Valley & Western) and abandonment.

Whatever the farmers thought of Jim Hill, they took his advice to raise more wheat. The land was available, the soil was right, the weather and rainfall conditions were right, and there seemed to be little risk. Wheat was easily shipped and was marketable. Settlers answered the call of the plow. Jim Hill had opened the plains to the plow and profits. His promise of the promised land had been fulfilled.

North Dakota soon ranked as one of the world's largest producers and exporters of wheat, most of which moved to market aboard the trains of the GN. Wheat, and more wheat; not even Jim Hill could have imagined the annual harvest nor the endless parade of grain trains moving over his line. More wheat than he dreamed possible.

The stunning scenery of a field of ripening wheat is a beautiful sight and can be overwhelming. With the wind rustling through the grain, the undulating fields stretch for miles. The heads are fat and healthy. Jim Hill, "the Empire Builder," created billions of dollars in new wealth. He enhanced the value of the land, he converted vast untaxable acres into taxable properties, and he helped to unite and solidify the state. The immense direct benefits arising from the "Empire Builder" are beyond measurement, and the indirect benefits are still being felt today. It has been said that other regions of the nation had been settled by the ox cart, but the "Hill Country" was settled by the boxcar.

The railroad depot always provided a sense of community identification. Many "town" sites never went into operation; they were "still born"—never developed. Many did not have a depot, some had a post office, which usually closed in a few years, but all had a side track, and maybe an industrial track that may not have ever been used.

North Dakota was shaped by the lay of the tracks, which established the towns, the routes to markets and the flow of the population. The shape of the state was thus determined when it was admitted into the union in 1889.

Adventurous motorists can drive alongside Jim Hill's railroad and imagine themselves at the head end of one of his trains. It is an exhilarating journey westward across the high plains. One can imagine the passing of people and trains of long ago, while the ghost of Jim Hill glances momentarily in the dim light of his business car as he rushes purposefully to do battle with other giants of the railroad world.

Jim Hill and his Great Northern were truly the architects of North Dakota. He said upon his retirement in 1912, "Most men who have really lived, have had, in some shape their great adventure. This railway is mine. I made my mark on the face of the earth and no man will ever wipe it out. When we are all dead and gone, the sun will still shine, the rains will fall and this railroad will run as usual." Jim Hill, the "Empire Builder" would be proud to see what his railroad did for the development of the state. As the one-eyed railroad tycoon looks on, there is no doubt that this is his railroad, his trains, and his empire of wheat.

Jim Hill's avoidance of bankruptcy during the Panic of 1893, and later the 1929 crash, is a tribute to his genius. He was a financial wizard. He was able to weather the financial storm and the heavy cost of extending his railroad to Puget Sound. The GN was completed in 1893. The heavy cost of overbuilding of branch lines, mostly in North Dakota, and competition strained the resources for 10 years, following the crash of 1893. The GN's thread of steel rails was under-utilized. Jim Hill and his successors never had to face a bankruptcy judge. That his venture succeeded was good for him, good for the GN and for North Dakota, and it still is.

Sidings were named in chronological order as the NP built westward from Fargo, before settlement of the area. Fargo was first called "The Crossing" (of the Red River). Third Siding became Buffalo, Fourth Siding now Oriska and Fifth Siding grew into Valley City. Sixth Siding, 64 miles west of Fargo, became Hobart, but with no development, it was removed from the railroad's listing in 1925, as was Seventh Siding, Eckelson, and Eighth Siding; Tenth Siding and Burton did not survive. Spiritwood remains as a ghost town.

Death at an Early Age: Where Did the Tracks Go?

CONWAY FARED BETTER than other towns in northeastern North Dakota. It reached a peak population of 228 in 1890, but by 1980 there were 33 people left. Other "has beens" include Cashel, Auburn, Voss, Warsaw, Oak Ridge, Nash, Oakwood, Veseleyville and Ninth Siding. They cluster around Grafton like satellites circling the earth. The combined population of the ten "towns" is about 300. These "towns" are so obscure that nothing could be found about many of them, except that they were served by the BNSF, and all are now ghost towns. Even a rail line did little to save these towns.

Bowesmont is history. Following the devastating Red River flood in 1997, Pembina County, and the state and federal governments told the town to give up. The town had suffered too many floods, almost every year. The worst floods were in 1948, 1949, 1950, 1979, and the worst of all in 1997. All buildings were purchased by a federal buyout program, and buildings were moved away or destroyed. The people were forced out of their homes, which met the bulldozer. It never had many people; it was not shown on road maps. No population figures could be found.

The farming community was founded in 1878 by Icelanders. The tiny community had all the problems of small towns everywhere: depopulation and a dwindling trade base. It also had one big disadvantage: floods. The town was established when the Duluth & Manitoba Railroad

(D&M) extended a rail line 95 miles, from Grand Forks to Pembina, in 1887, and completing the line to Winnipeg in 1888. The D&M was absorbed by the Northern Pacific (NP) on June 5, 1893. It was this line that sparked the railroad war between the NP and GN Railroads, which raged for almost 100 years. The feud continued until the two merged in the 1970s, forming the Burlington Northern Railroad.

"It is the only instance of a plotted community to be deliberately eliminated as a result of the Red River floods," said Tom Isern, a North Dakota State University history professor. Bowesmont lasted 119 years.

Blabon died: will someone please turn out the lights? Once a thriving up-and-coming railroad town, founded when the GN built through here in 1896 on its way to Devils Lake, Blabon grew to almost 200 people. It never became a railroad center—it had a side track. The elevator closed years ago. It had some stores to line the tracks. Gilbert Johnson was the GN agent here for 50 years, from 1910 to 1960. Mr. Gilbert was born in 1876, nine years before the railroad built through here. Today it is a true ghost town, population 0. The road sign disappeared 20 years ago, and the town is no longer shown on road maps.

Ninety-year-old Ed Tranby was the last person to leave town, in October 1997. He closed the house and moved to an apartment in Cooperstown, some 30 miles away. For sixty

Here and there a ruined house or barn sits under flaking coats of paint, its roof buckling like a sway back of an old pack horse. The far-off horizon peeks through empty doors and window frames like a ghost world. This sway-back was found in Mooreton.

years he lived in the three-bedroom house, that he bought for $100 in 1937. He and his late wife raised five children in the house. Leaving is not easy. Edwin says he is moving back in the spring. He loves the spring and summer in Bladon, but winters get long, lonely and bleak. Edwin is not one to show his emotions, nor spill the contents of his heart. Vacant towns don't talk. It will be tough to know whether Edwin misses Bladon, or if Bladon misses Edwin. Loyalty runs deep.

Bladon was never much of a community, but finally it has a claim to fame. It is a town with no residents. Nothingness has been bearing down on Bladon for decades.

The line of settlements became a unbroken line on the prairie. In these abandoned towns, we find the true genesis of a ghost town.

Today, they are not shown on modern road maps, and the ghosts of early days walk the streets. The towns suffered greatly from the Great Depression. They lost out when the interstate high-

way bypassed them, but they survive as larger than normal ghosts of the prairie. The prophets of doom and gloom knew they would die.

Wildrice, Hickson, Lithia, Christine, Enloe, Abercrombie, Woodhill, Tyler and Blackmer came to life as the Fargo & Southern stabbed its track into the rich Red River Valley in 1884. It became the Milwaukee Road in 1885. Blackmer, five miles south of Fairmount, has disappeared. The elevator was razed in 1974, and no trace could be found of the community. Wildrice has found a new use for itself as a south suburb bedroom community for Fargo, home to the hard-working, middle-class urban refugees who have been priced out of the city. These small towns tasted the sweetness of success. They were on the map, their success was assured, and they thought they would live forever. Few regions had a network of rail lines as prolific as North Dakota. This proliferation led to redundancy, and redundancy led to abandonment.

Mooreton, once the center of a huge wheat

A building recycling project is under way on this Mooreton barn. Mooreton is trying to halt the slide into oblivion. It has a better reason to survive. It is the site of the Bagg farm, the last of the remaining "bonanza farms." The bonanza farms started in the 1870s and were common in North Dakota, promoted by the expanding Northern Pacific. Eventually the Bagg farm grew to 27,000 acres and another 32,000 acres in Steele County. Upon the death of the owner, Mr. Downing, in 1913, the farm became the property of Frederick Austin Bagg. Subsequent sales of land reduced the farm to average size, but the original buildings remain.

bonanza farm, was established in the 1870s–1880s, when the NP Railroad built through the Red River Valley, and along with nearby Dwight, faded from view. They were too close to Wahpeton. The people deserted them for greener pastures.

The opening of the north-south Interstate Highway 29 and the east-west Interstate Highway 94 was a major blow to the small communities. The highways destroyed hundreds of towns within 25 or so miles on either side of the freeway. Blame for urban sprawl and the destruction of the rural communities can be attributed to the automobile and cheap gasoline, the cheapest in the world. The design and development of the interstate highway infrastructure around the automobile was just another nail in the coffin.

The discontinuance of long distance transcontinental passenger trains caused the demise of regional feeder bus lines, providing a domino effect. Bus lines served as feeder lines to the trains at strategic locations, like a "spine and ribs" integrated system. Branch-line passenger trains had been discontinued many years earlier. Buses were substituted to replace them and to provide public service to outlying towns. They too would be discontinued as highways were improved. Air service took away the majority of the travel at the larger communities, leaving the "ghost" towns to the bus lines. The economic pressures forced them to quit.

Jackrabbit bus lines connected Winnipeg's two Canadian transcontinental railroads with Omaha, Nebraska. En route they served Grand Forks, Fargo (Fargo had a dozen passenger trains, in every direction), Wahpeton, and the South Dakota towns of Watertown, Brookings (a college town), Sioux

Falls, Sioux City, connecting the many bus routes and trains in Omaha in every direction.

When the trains stopped, the buses stopped too. Both faded into the pages of history. Feeder bus lines were the threads that stitched the state together after the passenger trains left the branch lines. But the passenger infrastructure unraveled, and the state is as isolated today as it was in the early settlement days when it comes to public transportation. The people are now dependent upon the automobile—no car, no travel. The loss of passenger service has had a devastating effect on the mobility of the rural population. The communities lost another battle for survival.

Americans have always been a nation on the move, an antsy republic of migrants and wanderers ready to pull up stakes after a crop failure or bad prices or the closing of a store or a farm. There always seems to have been the promise of a better life elsewhere. Among the casualties of our footloose ways are the countless small towns created in effusions of optimism, then simply abandoned when hope and time ran out.

It was less than practical to think that the numerous small towns in the area could survive. The economic connections and the markets were not assured in a region already dominated by larger towns. The Fargo/Wahpeton/Ortonville line of the Milwaukee Road was abandoned on November 3, 1979. A few buildings and a few people survive as well as a few memories in small towns along this line. The towns ended in the same manner as the Fargo & Southern. The yo-yo of hope goes downward more than upwards for these towns.

15

Will Eventually be a Railroad Center

FOR A WHILE, Overly was a railroad center. It was a crew change point and terminal for the trains. It had a roundhouse and all the businesses needed to serve a fledgling community. The prairie grasses have covered any remains of the roundhouse and turntable, and the hotel has fallen down, as have most of the other buildings. Daily trains are now but a memory, but a rich and multifaceted memory remains.

The depot was usually located on the edge of town. The popular activity was to watch the trains come into town when the engineer blew a long blast of the whistle. The populace flowed from main street to enjoy one half of the day's excitement. When the trains left in the morning, one train went east to Thief River Falls, the other went west to Kenmare. The other half was enjoyed when the trains came back in the evening. The populace was living in clover. Each train had to be met, whether work got done or not. The tobacco chewers congregated on the platform, where the men and boys engaged in telling "dirty stories" while the harried station agent—rushing to position the carts to load or unload baggage, mail, and express—had to chase them off. The engineer always stopped at exactly the correct spots.

The trains came into town in the evening, the local people making friends with a nameless engineer. After 1950, the trains didn't come into town at all. The depot was torn down; the old

steam locomotive and its roundhouse were melted into scrap. Overly's history, and its heart, were torn out, and it finally disappeared from the map. After the trains left, it had little reason to exist. Today, logic would seem to dictate that there is no good reason for any of the ghost towns to exist. Ten people call Overly home. The people who live here like it because it has no future; they don't have to worry about development.

Nekoma boomed when the military selected the town for a Safeguard Anti-Ballistic Missile site (ABM), a military radar installation. Workers flocked to the town for the high-paying jobs, rumored to be 3,000 in number. Housing was scarce, so people and the town went into debt to build houses and services. They spent millions. New fire trucks, new sidewalks, a new school, a playground, a swimming pool were acquired. The base cost $5.5 billion. Nekoma hit the jackpot. The missile site was completed and declared operational on October 1, 1975. One week later it was declared obsolete. The base closed before it ever became fully functional. The town emptied. There was no tax base. The fire truck sits unused and police cars do not roam the streets. Nekoma's fame was based on the ABM. It needed the military base to survive. In the Cold War the missile silo was a subterranean cash cow. The SALT I treaty made the base obsolete. The military was grounded, the base was grounded and

Clustered grain bins stand like lighthouses at the end of main street in Overly. With the wheat shipments, the town seemed to be well on its way to a prosperous future. The sun and the passage of time have taken their toll on main street. No traffic flows on the single-lane gravel street, no business is conducted, and little remains of this prairie town. This photo bears out that the end is near. Soon Overly will pass into the pages of history and will be forgotten.

The church closed down, then was converted into a repair garage, and it failed. Despite its years of emptiness, the building stands tall. But eventually it will fall down, the debris will be removed, and the grasses will grow back. A ghost appears as a double image, as a white shadow. The church has literally given up the ghost.

so was Nekoma. It was an instant ghost town. It was a settlement sustained by the Cold War, and it died in peace. Governments come and go, but the prairie endures. The grass comes back. In the struggle for life and death, the prairie remains impersonal.

Hove Mobile Park City (Hove City), six miles east of Nekoma, was built in 1966 to house workers. It grew along with Nekoma. But when the base closed in October 1975 the population fell, to 20 by 1980, and to two by 1997.

These towns have been dealt with at length because they symbolize the dream of westward expansion. All were established with lofty hopes, but all were doomed to extinction when the residents gravitated to the larger towns in the area.

Overly is typical of the small grain-gathering towns of the north country. They seemingly remain frozen in an earlier era of black and white movies. Only the bright red and white SOO LINE locomotives keep us in the present. The welcome sign says population 32, down from more than 300 in 1970, but today only ten call it home. Come back in a few years and see if the sign still stands and how many people will greet you. The quest today seems hard to equate with the towns' lively past.

For a while Overly was a railroad center; train crews changed here. As a terminal, it boasted a two-stall engine house, a turntable, coal and water facilities, and a number of related structures. The hotel has fallen down, the cafes have closed, the depot is gone, and the church no longer greets worshipers. Daily trains are now but a memory, but a rich and multifaceted history remains.

The Overly cafe specialized in home cooking, but no one has eaten a meal here in a long time. The ten people who live here, like it because it has no future and they don't worry about development. Today's logic would seem to dictate that there is little reason for the town to exist. Worn out by long hours and declining business, the cafe's owners threw in the towel.

Above the Mighty Mouse River

NORMA, Grano, Greene, Hurd, Eckman, Russell, Omemee, Overly, Fonda, Mylo, Agate, Calio, Allison, Loma, and Amourdale were all laid out in 1905 by the Tri-State Land Co., a development arm of the SOO LINE . The railroad map of North Dakota was now complete; this was the last railroad expansion in the state. All of these towns were seeking fame and fortune. It was thought they would blossom like the rose.

Mylo's population peaked at 140 in 1920, then dropped to 31 by 1980. By 1990 it was dead. Armourdale skyrocketed to 25 people in 1930, and remained on most road maps into the 1960s, then disappeared. Services were available in Elsberry, then boasting 15 people, itself a ghost. Little Chicago of the West, later given the more manageable name of Dunseith, would soon rival the great city in Illinois. It didn't make it. The promotional rhetoric accompanying the settlement inspired many of the small towns to label themselves as "capital" of something.

Spur 562, four miles west of Columbus, was used for the shipment of grain and cattle. It was named to note the distance west of Minneapolis by the SOO LINE. It has disappeared, as has Strange Siding and Niobe.

Antler (population 39) and Loraine (population 21) at the top of the state close to the Canadian border, died when the railroad abandoned its tracks. Few buildings remain in the grizzled ghost towns. Much like the price of farm products dur-ing the Depression, the settlements were fragile. They were crushed by the various economic and social changes occurring in the region. Bad weather, crop failures, and perhaps a love for the larger cities drew most of the residents away.

Antler was spawned in 1898 when the GN built an 80-mile branch line from Rugby to the Canadian border. It grew for a while, just like Chicago, which was also the "end of track." It would be an international gateway; goods and passengers would flow to and fro.

By the 1960s Antler was dying. Many businesses had closed, and the school was threatened to be closed. A few loyal old-timers refused to accept defeat. They stayed in town, ever hopeful that the town would be revived. They had watched the town spring to life as a border station into Canada, then watched as it slowly began to die. It was the historical nature of the town, mired in tradition, and in meeting the challenge head-on. Only a few saw the need for imaginative solutions to Antler's woes.

Harley "Bud" Kissner thought he had a solution when he offered 42 acres of land free to anyone who would move to Antler, raise a family, and stay for five years. His plan brought national attention. He was not a wealthy man, but he had a big heart and was concerned about the declining population and the school closure. Land was valued at $500 an acre. Sixty families answered the call, and seven were selected, those

Not much left to be proud of in Antler. The town is slipping away into the wheat fields.

Rebecca Lodge, a meeting place for Masons and Odd Fellows in Antler. The fire station still protects the town and nearby farms. Despite the legacy of Bud Kissner and the past presence of the railway in the town, very little survives to commemorate the formative period in the town's history.

with large families. They moved in with tents and mobile homes. Collectively the families had 26 children. BINGO! Antler found the answer to the pupil enrollment problem. It was a one-man, modern-day Homestead Act.

The town needed a welder and mechanic. Mike and Barbara Ellis moved from Utah, seeking serenity and space to raise their nine children. His new business flourished but there was trouble brewing. Antler did little to find suitable employment and adequate housing. The newcomers had to fend for themselves. Something went wrong. The business failed, they moved away, and Antler no longer had a welder. The newcomers were not made to feel welcome. The ultraconservative community looked at the newcomers as "welfare freeloaders."

Antler townsite is unusual. It is designed in what has been described as a "wagon wheel" pattern, featuring a prominent building at the hub, with tree-lined spoke-like streets spreading outwards. This hub building, at one time, housed the post office, the customs office, the city police, the mayors office, and the like, and apartments upstairs. A few main street buildings are of historical note, most notably the impressive building in the center of the village.

Fights broke out—one ended in a lawsuit. There were two divorces. The bitterness ran deep. The community was divided, and the wounds did not heal. Eventually it would destroy the town. All had moved away before the five years expired. Then it happened: The school closed in 1987, followed by the grocery store, the hardware store, the gasoline station and the Catholic church. The railroad took back 12 miles of its track, retreating to Westhope. There are shells of other buildings, which at one time held two banks, a doctor's office, a garage, and a Lutheran church. Bud Kissner was right when he said, "When the school bell goes silent, it's a powerful sign that one more small town is in the last stages of life." Antler's slide into oblivion is a personal sorrow for him. "I tried to make a difference," he said. " I tried." Emotions run deep. When the school closed it also closed the town. There is a post office and a bar/restaurant, but that is about all that is left. These stay open because of Canadians coming across the border to patronize them.

There is no possibility that the school bell will ever ring again in Antler. From the cradle to the grave, from birth to death, is all too typical of the once prosperous family farm towns withering on the dusty fields of the Great Plains.

Leona Tennyson of Antler and 7,000 North Dakota women achieved fame by making the world's largest quilt, for the 1989 North Dakota Centennial. It is featured each year at the North Dakota State Fair in Minot. It measures 134 feet-by-85 feet, and was featured in the 1993 Guinness Book of World Records. The record has since been surpassed by quilt makers in Canada and England, but for a brief moment in North Dakota history she and Antler found their place in the sun.

Hundreds of towns were established in the state in the bitter struggle between the railroads to gain territory. The state wound up with a density of towns that is far out of proportion to its population. Some of the dreams lived a brief and futile life, some flourished for a short time and then withered to tiny static landmarks fighting to maintain their place on the map. It was hard to predict which of the new sites would grow and which would die.

We never hear of the loss of the small towns

Antler. Mr. William Wegner operated a jewelry store and Albert Ladux ran a hardware store (the building is now used as a community hall). Meat was sold in the building on far left.

because they do not fit our picture of urban troubles. As a rural event, it is outside our normal expectation and has faded from our communal memory. Small towns may be seen as hicksville to some of the larger cities in North Dakota and in other states but to those who lived and still live there, they are a major part of their life, and hold strong memories.

Many early settlements relied on cattle for milk and meat, and started cheese factories to market the excess milk. Every farm had a few milk cows and normally produced more milk than could be consumed by family and animals. Inadequate transportation prevented the shipping of raw milk any distance. The only solution was to produce cheese and butter, which could be transported a greater distance (2000 pounds of milk produced 200 pounds of cheese). Creameries and small cheese makers filled a local need, employed local people and yielded a useful product. Eventually, strict sanitary laws, competition from larger more efficient cheese factories, and

the Great Depression forced the small town factories to give up. Modern, more efficient methods drove the small cheese factories out of business. Today, North Dakota dairy farms are few. The herds are large, and huge bulk milk trucks roam the country roads carrying the milk to distant places.

There was too much railroad track. There were too many small towns. Many hamlets had two railroads; the towns and railroads were on a treadmill. Every new settler demanded more services. As they produced more wheat, more track was built, and another town was established. Then more settlers arrived, and round and round it went. Feeder lines dominated the expanding rail network. The rail companies endorsed the concept of "density of branch lines," calling them "gathering lines."

Towns rose overnight with the advancing track and the push of the settlers. As towns and farms were built around the railroad as "flimsy little wooden shacks," they became ubiquitous. As more and more "towns" were established by

A Mr. Hughs ran this Farmers Union gasoline station in Antler and lived in the house behind it. It was not forced out of business by competition, but by lack of customers. The tracks, the railroad station, and the stores are gone with little in their place, except potholed streets and nondescript buildings.

building into remote undeveloped country, the chance of their success was diminished.

An optimist would call the expansion a bet on the future. A realist would call it a hopeful expedition into undeveloped prairie land. A cynic would call it a fantastically expensive exercise in ego gratification.

The winners and losers in the great civic shifting were evident from the start. There are restless ghosts still seeking the security of being on the map. The places yo-yoed from relative boom to relative bust. They had received their death sentences. History will soon forget these places.

The geographical difference between the population centers of the 1990s, is not much different than a hundred years ago, but most everything in between is gone. The rapidity of movement that we know today between the scattered towns has made the small towns obsolete. The relationship between then and now, past and present, is always shifting. These forces worked simultaneously to cause overbuilding, and the boom times could not last.

The interstate highways seem barren of identity. Built for speed, they either defaced, destroyed or bypassed the towns, accepting no responsibility for the damage done to the American scene. The landscape succumbed to the concrete apron, taking 40 acres of land for every mile. Today, the interstates siphon off much of the traffic so most of the time we had the backroads to ourselves, going for hours without seeing another car. We felt like motorists from the 1930s. Sometimes it is hard to stay off the freeways. Often that old road serves as a frontage road, and suddenly the poky little road turns into an on-ramp. There are no ghost towns on the interstate highways.

Cheap gasoline contributed to the demise of the small town. It allowed people to travel greater distances at minimum costs to shop in larger cities. Gasoline is not taxed like other developed countries, where gasoline taxes are five times higher than in the United States. It is ironic that in an era of unprecedented economic growth, these towns should have a survival problem. A war in

This farm house follows the trend of Antler. It sits and waits for total destruction by weather, lightning strikes, a tornado or vandals. The end is inevitable.

the oil producing countries and a huge increase in gasoline prices will devastate the state, and will bring the state and the nation to its knees, faster than any natural disaster. Half of U.S. oil consumption is provided by foreign producers. In such key areas as fuel, the U.S. should never put itself in the vulnerable position of depending on a cheap supply from a foreign source. It is inevitable that there will come a time when the ever-expanding highways built to suit ever-larger vehicles will not look so inviting.

To promote fuel efficiency (smaller cars, fewer gas-guzzling monsters) and the use of alternate fuels when oil is freely flowing and cheaply, is a hard sell. But it is something we will have to face, if the Middle East should erupt again, as it did in 1973. The stability of the volatile Mideast is sub-ject to instant reversal. The oil reserves in the U.S. are 566 million barrels, equal to a 67-day supply, and that will drop to a 46-day supply by the year 2002. Strategists fear a "collision" with a transportation disaster.

Interstate 29 runs north and south through the eastern quarter of the state. A traveler on an interstate gains speed but loses contact with the details of the surrounding countryside. The details of the land through which they run and the people who live along them can only be experienced by driving through North Dakota's outback. The smaller highways, like twisting veins that wander through each town and slip into the valleys, gave us time to smell the fragrance of the landscape, to mosey along and get the flavor of whatever area we were in.

Home is Where the Heart Is: But the Heart Cannot Go Home

WHEN WE WERE YOUNG, most of us believed our homes were uninteresting and lifeless; we left as soon as possible. Often, as we mature, we return for values we didn't appreciate as youths: clean air, pure but scarce water, open spaces, and prairie beauty.

In our time, history moves in geometric progression. In a 20-year period (1970–1990) the life of the towns probably changed more radically than in any single proceeding generation, and all individuals have changed. Maturity cannot pass these lessons to future generations. It is nature's secret way of preserving the idealism of youth, as a source spring of human maturity through trial and error.

Interstate Highways 94 and 29 and U.S. Highways 2, 10 and 83 get all the glory, but the truly magical American roads are the less traveled backroads, the blue highways on the road maps. For 50 years the U.S. and state highway system formed the country's premier high-speed, all-weather road network.

We see the interstates clogged with cars, as though the whole thing has been designed by some diabolical force bent on making human beings miserable. The highway strip is not just a sequence of eyesores. The pattern it represents is also economically catastrophic, an environmental calamity, socially devastating and spiritually degrading.

Will the prairie continue to be choked with billboards and will the interstates turn their backs on the rich heritage found on the prairie? Will the prairie fight to maintain its uniqueness, es-

chewing the golden arches and insisting instead on the real golden empire?

These are the questions uppermost in my mind as I wrestled to understand how it was that we lost our heritage. Like any cataclysm, the loss of rural populations awakens one's interest in the process. The rural population historically embraced, then forsook, a genuine commitment to preserve its natural heritage.

Regrettably, the first casualties of the improved highway system was the small town business. As people retreated to the privacy of their own cars they lost the sense of community, and identity. The remaining small towns between the larger communities are sleepy or dying hamlets that are heavily dependent on farming. Some towns are poor and derelict, reflecting the hard realities of economics in wheat country.

The interstates did not care about the damage they had inflicted on the fabric of the towns. Cheap gasoline keeps the people moving to larger communities. Air travel, trucking, and automobiles took their toll. The loss of dozens of passenger trains, hundreds of miles of branch lines, and the loss of thousands of small town jobs were fatal.

North Dakota has not benefited from the exodus of people moving out of California. The new settlers are seeking what settlers have always wanted—space—physical and psychic breathing room. North Dakota has all of these but not many off-season NBA coaches or broadcast tycoons are buying North Dakota acres. It isn't too difficult to

A number of people have left Voss for greener pastures, and left a ghost. The place is losing its grip on life and is not shown on road maps. Farmers represent a way of life that is becoming a way of death—a dying ghost. Located on two unmarked county/township roads, Voss is north and west of Grand Forks. The town is on the Fargo/Grand Forks line of the BNSF, and there are few residents to see or hear the traffic. The spot has disappeared from road maps.

There is not much to tell about Kelso. The tracks streak through town, reaching for a more important destination. Note that the elevator has closed and the side loading track was removed. Kelso could not be a grain - gathering center, even if it wanted to.

locate these isolated town sites. They are best found by a ground search aided by a detailed map.

"If you're not on an interstate highway or do not have a major merchandising center with a major anchor like a Wal-Mart, the chances of survival is questionable," said one local resident. "Wal-Mart and other discounters are the innovators; they are the experts in marketing. They are able to go into a middle-sized community and make it into a major shopping center. It is usually enough to assure the survival of the town," she said.

As larger communities expanded into K-Marts and Wal-Marts, these retailers conducted a vigorous public relations campaign to win the citizens, stating, "We're on your side, we're here to work with you. We want to help your community. We want to be good neighbors." They wanted all the business themselves; they allowed local businesses in the downtown areas to be dismantled and destroyed.

Tiny Taft sits and sits on an unmarked county road along the Fargo/Grand Forks line of the BNSF. In many "ghosts" the only business is a grain elevator. Only a handful of people ever called this place home, or probably ever will.

The presence of discount superstores can make things more difficult for the smaller retail business. Because of their size, they are able to purchase in large volumes, which allows them to offer a wider variety of items, which attracts shoppers who dislike shopping at several different places. They offer a discount price and sell in large quantities. Wal-Mart has reshaped retailing and brought it to a new level of merchandising. The new business source also gives Wal-Mart a greater hold on the economics of many small towns. Such is the nature of capitalism.

It is a principle of economics that only the strong survive. The cream of the crop do best, whether individuals, stores or towns. In Wal-Mart, as in America, the tension between competing values can be fascinating. Patriotism is not always compatible with the commitment to low prices. Pressed with tough economic times, shoppers place value ahead of loyalty, but for the shoppers Wal-Mart and other discounters have proven to be a salvation. "Loyalty from my customers left when Wal-Mart came through the door," said one merchant.

The rush to suburbia is pushed by any farmer willing to sell his wheat and cornland and become a millionaire ex-farmer. Farmland is being paved over with thousands of miles of new streets, new highways, airports, industrial parks, and Wal-Mart parking lots, connecting thousands of new housing developments with the huge shopping malls. Fat, rich America sprawls over a far-flung landscape accessible only by the auto.

Like America itself, the big box stores excite strong reactions. People are wary of the superpower. They mistrust its motives, fear its cultural clout, deride its brashness, yet marvel at its convenience and admire its success. As with America, the people keep coming and buying.

Main street in Kelso. A few buildings, a few stores, a few people, a few grain bins nestled to the tracks, and a church are all that remains.

Picturesque Buxton. Main Street is laid out opposite the railroad tracks as in most of the prairie townsites. The bank represented stability through its solid physical facility. Buxton is a mute reminder of the flourishing era when this town was in its glory with a population of 410. The BNSF tracks run through the heart of town, but the heartbeat is not strong. Times are so tough," says a sign on the Buxton grain elevator, the closest thing to a public square in a pin-dot prairie town like this, "that even the people who don't intend to pay aren't buying." It is a bit of black humor, but not too many people are laughing.

Buxton was one of our surprises, a viable elevator loading a covered hopper and a box car. An operating elevator helps to keep a small town from dying. Budd Reeve, a prolific writer, obtained the townsite from the railroad in exchange for the land used for the old Union Depot in Minneapolis, Minnesota. He named the town for his friend, Minneapolis Treasurer Thomas J. Buxton.

Before Niobe was deserted in the 1960s, '70s, and '80s, its population of several hundred carved a colorful niche in the state's history. The population grew, but it lost out to other nearby towns and the change in the railroad's operations. It is an idyllic setting where the pace is slow and nobody keeps tab on the population figures.

Probably the most imposing sight along Highway No. 200 is the James River Landmark Lutheran church and cemetery, west of Carrington. Occasionally a pioneer is laid to rest in the well-maintained cemetery. The lofty spire of the church can be seen for miles. Folks for miles around pooled their resources and labor to build this church, which seats more people than there are in the surrounding countryside.

In its glory days, Niobe was a busy place. Trains were dispatched from this junction to Crosby, to the west, and to North Gate on the Canadian border. The depot stands in testimony to an earlier era when passenger trains stopped here, taking people to other train connections and on to civilization. At this writing, Niobe is little more than a hamlet, with only a signpost, a siding, and one grain elevator. Once the depot was a busy place. It had an engine house where engines were prepared to work the branch lines, and the yard sorted out the cars. All that activity is gone. A small, unusual church, now vacant, is a symbol of its heyday. From a peak population of 250 in the '20s, the town saw a rapid decline in the 30s and virtually disappeared by 1995. The depot is worth the stop. A maintenance-of-way crew uses the depot as a mini storage warehouse.

Nature has reclaimed most of its domain in the bluestem gamma grass prairie, although a small elevator dominates this scene in Niobe.

Coteau (French for hills) is known as the "biggest little town in North Dakota." The schoolhouse is empty for the summer. Will the children be back come fall? Many towns have given up their status as a village to save on property taxes. Doing away with the "city" status, they qualify for agricultural tax exemption, a lower rate.

Larson, a Pygmy of a place of 21 people or fewer. Odds are that the town will not survive, losing out to more convenient towns nearby. A handful of people still live here, and generally do not roam far from the home on the range.

The photo of the wooden elevator at Noonan was taken June 13, 1991. Like soldiers guarding the border, wooden elevators dot the landscape. This small wooden elevator was killed by the large grain giants: concrete silos (mailing tube), the railroad covered hopper and unit grain trains. Wooden soldiers are alike in their uniformity. Small elevators line the road beds of the rail lines, like soldiers at attention.

Same Town—Different Name: Cookie Cutter Communities

TO THE CASUAL TRAVELER, the small towns of North Dakota, regularly spaced about eight to ten miles apart, can seem mundane and unremarkable. On the prairie there are no strange attractions, no rich man's mansion. Instead there is wheat, the land is simplicity itself, and it has been that way for a long time.

Most communities welcomed the interstate highway system, fervently believing it would make each little town grow larger. Instead the opposite was true. The highway made it easier for tourists and locals alike to go to the next larger town. Big billboards reflect community desperation for business, and the age and run-down condition of local businesses show that it is already too late. Many of the towns have ceased to be real communities offering diverse services and entertainment that reflect the preference, nationalities and interests of the local citizens. Now they're simply strips of fast food joints, gasoline stations and convenience shops. One town is hard to distinguish from another.

Each sleepy hamlet has its constellation of churches, grain elevators and streets. They all had the same residential pattern to the point where they almost look as if they were created with a cookie cutter. The early settlers nestled next to the tracks, the main street running perpendicular to the track. The first business was usually a grain elevator and the town grew near and around it.

They were born over a century ago and settled by colonies of God-fearing people seeking the American dream in the prairie Mecca. But the riches they sought are long gone.

For centuries, lightning fires kept the grasslands free of scrubs. The prairie undergoes a purging fire frequently. The grass and wildflowers return, but most of the undesirable weeds and bushy growth are turned to ash. So it is with ghost towns. Fire consumed many of the ghosts and most were not able to rise again.

Grass, knee-high, and waving like the ocean, is the staff of life. In any weather it is easy for the casual visitor to imagine the prairie as an empty sea. Even from a distance or even a hundred yards, the prairie takes on a sameness of unjudgeable depths. Nature may not be in charge of prairie fires any more—they are usually controlled. For lovers of grass, this is as good as it gets.

Every tiny whistle stop had dreams of becoming a "new Chicago." Every town had the identical set of businesses, a general store, a butcher shop, a couple of saloons, probably a hotel, a bank, a school, and a newspaper. Far from the major distribution centers, the closely spaced towns competed with each other for the little business available, but they could not compete against their larger neighbors. As a result, the hamlets that were least favorably located reached their peak early in their life and declined thereafter.

The smaller towns became superfluous as the economic system passed them by. Just as the larger cities are struggling to deal with the loss of their industrial base, so too are the smaller towns scrambling to find new niches in the economic landscape. Nevertheless, the old towns are melting away too fast. Fires, drought and the Great Depression combined to bring the towns to their knees. Most were not able to rise from the ashes fully again.

Soon most of these reminders of the past will be gone, victims of the relentless, malevolent, ravenous gnawing of time. Few have found refuge from the human hammering of history. The possibility of being driven away is not a modern phenomenon. People have been relocating since the dawn of history. The drumbeat of the realities of the past, present, and future drove many of the footloose towards uncharted directions, new challenges, new dreams. Not only did the towns shrink smaller, many disappeared.

While it is easy to mourn the passing of the small towns, it must be pointed out that some reduction in the number of farm communities has been inevitable from the day the town plots were laid out. It is impossible not to feel some sense of loss as more and more towns disappear.

Many are deserted, overgrown with weeds, while others have become bustling centers that give no hint of their early past. Hundreds of others, not quite ghost towns but with little population, are quiet little towns tucked away on gravel roads.

Odd Names of Towns and How They Got Them

WOULD YOUR HOMETOWN, by any other name, seem the same? A town's name frequently suggests stories, legends, and romance. It is said that by your name you shall be known. So it is with towns. Sometimes a town's "handle" came from the poetic dreamer's pencil. It is likewise true of Seven Trees, named after a nearby grove of seven cottonwood trees on the open prairie. The love of a father for his daughter lives on in Amy. Arvilla was named after the founder's wife; Amanda's founder also honored his wife by naming the town after her. Willdo was a pun to complement its county seat of Cando. Wildo didn't do it. The town disappeared before the turn of the century. Stump was named for the prehistoric forest protruding from the waters of a nearby lake.

Travelers often search, in vain, for Geck, Lippert, Dengate, and have searched with equal futility for Vanhill, Coryell or Dexboro. Ong was named after the first postmaster in 1902. The post office closed in 1912, and the site disappeared. Why Not was an answer to inquiries about erecting a store building and the name was painted on the storefront to attract attention. Bicycle was named in recognition of the popular two-wheeled vehicle.

Nameless was given the name after postal officials rejected the first six names chosen, and Ops was named for the Roman goddess of plenty, who was the wife of Saturn and lived on the earth to protect agriculture. Bonetrail, a true ghost, was on the trail used by wagons to haul buffalo bones to Williston. It had a suburb, West Bonetrail, but only a small store was the extent of development.

The intent and humor of Done Workin' Beach is obvious, and Arthur was named for President Chester Alan Arthur in 1881. This town reversed the trend of dying communities—the town has had a steady growth and remains secure.

Dog Tooth was a stage stop on the Bismarck/Deadwood trail in 1877, named for a range of sandstone buttes, that resemble the molars of a dog's lower jaw. The site almost died after the stage line quit but was resurrected when the Milwaukee Railroad built its line to New England. It was renamed Raleigh.

Hoe was founded in 1907 and named for the common garden tool when the community could not agree on a name. The hoe lasted longer than the town for it was discontinued in 1908. Squaw Gap was named to note a local rock formation said to resemble an Indian squaw with papoose. It achieved national attention in 1971 when it became the last region in the nation to receive telephone service.

Nosodak on the west bank of the Missouri River was to be a construction camp on the proposed Northern Pacific line from Mandan to Galveston, Texas. The dream of a north-south transcontinental line died in 1914. The town lasted about 30 years until it was flooded by the waters of Lake Oahe. The name was coined from NOrth/SOuth DAKota to note its location.

The names of some North Dakota towns and communities reflect the flavor of the Old Country. Warsaw, New Hradee, Bremen, Hamburg, Viking, Walhalla, Bottineau, Kulm, Berlin, Norwegian, and Norway, show a strong bond to their old countries. Whiskey Point, south of Bismarck, was a spot to note the availability of liquor. Scandinavians like to drink; they are people, too.

Early town planners may not have used much originality in selecting names for their towns, but often were named for someone or something that was familiar to them, which made them seem more like "home."

20

More Than Tumbling Down: The Long Decline

LIKE HUNDREDS OF SMALL TOWNS across the U.S., North Dakota's small towns lost their confidence in the '70s and '80s. They lost their grip on the America ideal, and they looked around for the source of their discontent. Among the obvious and tangible objects of their wrath were the interstate highways, which bypassed them, the airlines, which flew over them, and the railroads, which abandoned them. These events were the final nails in the coffins of small towns. The economy of the small town isn't only depressed, it is being demolished.

Towns that once had two railroads vying for their business today cannot even flag down a Greyhound bus. In the midst of plenty, rural America is going out of business. The land has changed dramatically in the last decades; indeed, it has been changing for 50 years, since the Great Depression. Grand Forks, Minot, and Fargo were transfer points for many travelers in the early days, but now only one Amtrak train crosses the state, and it does so in the middle of the night, making a minimum number of stops. Only the large cities have air service, and it can be a long drive from many areas of the state to an airport. Airlines are expensive, charging as much as $2 a mile to get to a major connection such as Minneapolis or Denver. Automobiles are the main form of transportation for residents of the state—they give people mobility, and schedules don't have to be met.

Compounding the trials of small towns is the fact that there are fewer and fewer farmers every year. Half a century ago, when farmers were restricted to horse and wagon and muddy roads, towns had to be closely spaced. A community that served about 900 farmers in a 72-square-mile area was economically viable. Even in those days there were too many towns in relation to the rural population they served. Today, when a farmer can travel at least 60 miles in an hour to trade in a larger community, where prices may be cheaper and the selection of goods better, a marketing community must serve a 3,200-square-mile area that has a population of at least 26,000 to be economically successful.

The era of the small town on the prairie is over. While some have survived until the 1980s, those that remain usually have a roadside bar, and maybe a grain elevator. They lasted about 70 years. However, their importance has been declining since the 1920s because even then the auto and highways were beginning to undermine the place of the small town in community life. After World War II, car ownership and a rapidly improved road network quickly cut into the community business. This may not be in our comfort zone but the great prairie went through an economic and social revolution.

In town after town, schools closed and police and fire departments were consolidated with those in nearby villages. Bank branches were removed and countless other businesses were lost. With fewer customers to serve, there was less reason for businesses to maintain their stores.

We asked people why their town failed, and got a variety of answers: Interstate highways, super shopping centers that forced small stores out of business, cheap gasoline that made travel to larger communities possible, towns clustered too close together, the closing of schools, and trucks with cheaper freight rates that forced railroads out of business. People also said that their town died because large silo elevators forced out small elevators, passenger trains and business withdrew service, jumbo grain cars and unit grain trains were introduced, federal revenue sharing was eliminated, federal price supports were cut back, military bases closed (such as the ABM base in Nekoma), transportation was deregulated and farm mechanization lead to fewer farms. The reasons why there are ghost towns in North Dakota, of course, include all of the above.

Then there are those who said, "our town isn't dead!"

21

Winds of Change: The Price of Progress

SOMEONE ONCE SAID, "Change always comes, but most of us fail to recognize that it comes much faster than we realized it would."

During the 1970s, Congress grew increasingly concerned about the deteriorating railway system. Too many lines were bankrupt. Some had paid the ultimate price of liquidation, and others were on the verge of total collapse. They were in a financial straitjacket. There were too many nonproductive branch lines, too many small towns, too many one-railroad, one-car-at-a-time shippers. The rail system infrastructure was in shambles. The result was the Staggers Act, which deregulated railroads, airlines, buses and trucks.

One of the factors in the plight of the troubled towns is the deregulation of transportation. Airlines and buses pulled out, railroads discontinued the station agents and depots, then eventually abandoned the nonproductive branch lines; consequently, the towns lost their daily contact with the world. Branch lines and depots did not receive much attention after the Staggers Act was passed, and the railroads began a program of downsizing. The lines, which had long ago lost any economic reason to exist, were on the "hit list." These lines wasted freight cars, manpower, and diesel fuel.

When officials of one railroad asked the engineering department if a certain branch line could carry a 100-ton grain car they replied, "Yes, sir. You can run one but you will never run two." When a traffic study concluded that a conversion to heavier rail was not justified, the line was abandoned. They had functioned as a commercial lifeline for decades.

The fear of losing essential rail service, the direct result of deregulation and mergers and the dominance of giant rail systems, caused a worry about the future. The health of the agricultural economy depends on dependable rail service at reasonable grain freight rates. The takeover of the SOO LINE by the Canadian Pacific leaves the state with two giant rail systems. The future of transportation of North Dakota's agriculture will be decided in Montreal or Fort Worth instead of Minneapolis. The grain business is held captive because there is no competition.

Given today's economic environment, the branch lines are a financial burden on the larger companies because they earn less than it costs to operate. The money could be better spent on improving other parts of the system. Local industrial managers and shippers on marginal lines would like to operate the lines, but are not in any position to do it. Significant industrial development, businesses that ship regularly by rail, would need to take place before its future as a community freight hauler is assured.

Only emergency repairs and maintenance are being performed on the marginal lines. Trestles and

Nekoma's fate was based on the Anti-Ballistic Missile (ABM). The Cold War missile base was a subterranean cash cow. Built in the 1970s, it was to house about 3,000 military people. A huge housing infrastructure was built; Nekoma was in the big league. A week after the base was completed, the Salt II Treaty made it obsolete, and the entire complex was closed. Nekoma became an instant ghost town.

small bridges are usually constructed of wood; some date back to the 1920s and earlier. The bridge timbers are weak and rotting. The track is usually not ballasted and the ties are in bad condition.

Of all the crises affecting the state the loss of rail service is probably the most serious. Elevator operators, lumber yard managers and other merchants thought the railroad would be there forever, now began to read sadly about abandonments, mergers, short lines, and large-scale consolidations. They began to worry about the shrinking and changing transportation infrastructure. What if the plans go through? How would it effect my farm, my business? How would it effect my markets? The answer was, adversely. From Crosby to Grand Forks, from Fargo to Bismarck, from Minot to Mott, the new deregulation policy would seriously affect the state and the future of the small towns. Regional farmers sell their grain through large corporations that can manipulate prices and buy the grain wherever they get the best price. Shocked people, who heretofore paid scant attention to what was happening to their rail service, now began to

worry. But it was too late. The battle between the small communities and the faraway railroad headquarters would ultimately have great and grave consequences for both.

"We need rail access to world markets," said one elevator operator. "We can use trucks for the short term and the short haul, but we need the railroads for future growth. We are dead without them. We don't want to lose the spirit of competition, yet we want to capitalize on cooperation. That is the only way we are going to survive. Rail officials say it will cost an estimated $200,000 a mile to upgrade a line to handle heavy grain cars, versus $1 million a mile to upgrade a highway to handle heavy trucks. The trucks are pounding our roads to pieces. The investment in track upgrading seems like a good idea."

Farmers and towns must shake off the notion that railroad companies are a hindrance to their business, that the rail companies are not an adversary. They must cooperate if they want to succeed. No cooperation means no rail service, which leads to abandonment, and the towns lose. They can't

This barn is out of service. The old warrior has succumbed to the many years of heavy snow. It cannot even rest on its rotting timbers. It sits in the rich Red River Valley near Ardock.

have it both ways. There must be an agreement between the two; the future of both are tied together. They both succeed or both fail. That thought puts knots in the stomachs of elevator operators and industrial managers. It is frightening. The maneuver to preserve essential service does not ensure success, it only postpones the inevitable. They still live on the cutting edge of disaster.

The 1970s saw the beginning of a rationalization of the grain handling system. As older elevators reached the end of their economic life, they were removed and often were not replaced. Numerous towns thus lost their most important economic function, that of being a grain gathering point. While many of the villages have managed to survive as "convenience shopping centers," such communities have little need for all the business services provided by the larger towns.

Economics is an exact science. It is a cruel, unforgiving master. It shows no favoritism. For decades the 40-foot boxcar was the standard rail vehicle for the shipment of grain. Under the valid

assumption that what moves in a boxcar can also be carried in a covered hopper, and as cargo shifted to other vehicles (piggyback, containers, auto racks, lumber A frame flat racks, etc.) the boxcar was less and less useful, and was held in reserve for the annual peak grain harvest. Wholesale scrapping of the boxcar led to a "boxcar shortage." Branch line abandonment and the rationalization of grain handling had much to do with the inability of the boxcar to compete in the present market. Grain terminals in the major cities would only handle covered hoppers, usually weighing 100 tons each, and the light branch line track could not carry the heavy loads.

The 1980s brought more crises: tumbling land values, farm foreclosures, two droughts, school consolidations, deregulation and declining service, brain drain, loss of jobs caused by mechanization and increased use of cheap Third World labor. The result has been an exodus to urban centers.

As industry after industry is forced to realign their inventory and production runs, they demand smaller, faster and more frequent deliveries. They use the carrier's vehicles as a rolling warehouse. The boxcar was too labor intensive; shippers demanded piggyback and/or containers, or covered hoppers.

The container and piggyback highway trailer revolutionized the distribution delivery system. Trucks now deliver the piggyback trailers from railroad yards, eliminating the need to run a train on rickety track. The killing of the ICC sealed the fate of hundreds of miles of branch lines and with it uncounted elevators and line side settlements. Specialized covered hopper grain cars continue to be the vehicle of choice for the grain shipper. The end of the boxcar will come when the present fleet wears out, as shippers and carriers change to specialized rail cars. The boxcar will soon be obsolete.

With the introduction of the 100-ton grain covered hopper car, (now the 140-ton hopper), the rules of the grain handling business changed, and the players were different. It would change the landscape of the state. Grain terminals changed to handle the new railroad cars and this change did not include boxcars. Elevators were encouraged to load multi-car shipments (50-car unit trains). Shipping rates were reduced substantially. The economics of the covered hopper could not be ignored. The unit train became more attractive after the passage of the Staggers Act and spurred the development of the silo type (mailing tube) elevator.

Elevators loading a single 50-ton boxcar could not compete; they were forced to close. As the elevators closed, and the branch lines retired, the boxcars that served them were retired too. The boxcar was dead and it took the small elevator and the towns to the grave with it. The lonely elevators, and the 50-ton boxcar, were being crushed under the sheer weight of a heavy covered hopper grain car.

The main rail lines are still there. Some have been upgraded to handle heavier loads; others have been shortened, and some abandoned, but most are still in place doing the job they were built to do. This is granger country and the need to transport the grain has not changed, the distances have not changed, but the economics have. Huge grain silos now dominate the scene, placed about 100 miles apart. Grain shipments are consolidated from outlying areas by truck and loaded into rail unit trains for shipment to distant points. Truck hauling is cost-effective for about 50 miles.

Grain shippers now bid for grain cars, much like at an auction sale. The highest bidder over freight rate, offering the most carloads and the longest distance hauled, gets the cars. The small one- two- or three-car shippers cannot compete. They are literally forced out of business. The bid process is good for the large grain shippers loading 50 to 100 cars at a time. They are assured of grain cars when they need them, and the railroad is assured of a steady business and can plan its car distribution. It is good for both. This plan has virtually eliminated the annual "grain car shortage," and has shifted the burden, or blame, of car shortages to the shipper.

New grain loading incentive programs and the increasing abandonment of grain elevators will inevitably lead to more abandonments in the future. Communities scheduled to lose their businesses protested. Small town "boosterism" continued to thrive, indicating personal and community pride. A lot of people complain about the loss of small-town business, but they are the ones who drive 50 miles to shop in a larger community. If they want to support the small town, they need to do more than talk about it. They have to consider their values and the politics of shopping elsewhere. By making informed conscious decisions about what to buy and where to buy it, shoppers can ensure that the business community remains varied, colorful and thriving.

The number of country towns has declined since World War II, and this trend will likely continue as new methods of transportation, communication and the general economic change makes them obsolete. As the economic net tightens more businesses will close. Massive abandonment of rail lines will continue to occur into the 1990s and into the next century. The future of these small towns is predictable. They will die.

Today's survival has been easier for those small towns that have devised new purposes for themselves. For most towns, survival means diversification. Prosperity can no longer come from "beef and grain." It must come from industries that drive the national economy. Towns that have a sturdy physical infrastructure and a solid, established industrial base may survive, but all others will "implode," collapse into themselves.

"We hear a lot about rural development," said a cafe coffee drinker, "but it isn't going to happen. They think a General Motors or a major factory will drop a plant on them. We do not have the infrastructure to handle any more than 100 people. That is the common mistake rural folks make."

North Dakota is big enough to hold more people, but these settlers cannot live the "sweet" life until the planners create an economic atmosphere compatible with controlled growth.

The key is to set physical limits to urban sprawl and to develop smaller satellite cities with clear boundaries and solid economic bases. Some cities are buying land around their cities to create a buffer zone, forcing people to live outside the city. The cutting edge of this in-migration has been the so called "white flight" of people and corporations. So hungry are the towns for any stability that they are willing to welcome any economic enterprise by allowing short-term tax breaks. Usually this method does not work, for when the tax breaks run out the enterprise moves to another town and another tax break.

Towns cannot survive if the residents don't move faster to meet the challenge. They have choices; they can learn the new game being played, or they can continue to walk the way they always have. If they vote to stay the same, they will become the very best player in a game no longer played. No matter how much they long for the way it used to be, it isn't going to be that way. Many will not survive the century.

Most towns have a difficult time buying a fire truck. How are they going to find the money to attract meaningful industry? That kind of progress stopped long ago. The citizens have progressively campaigned to save all sorts of remaining businesses. It is a quiet, and mostly unsuccessful, attempt to ensure the preservation of important businesses, public and private, all across the North Dakota landscape. Although most tourists stay on the freeways, many towns have mounted advertising campaigns to lure travelers to the "scenic route" and to experience the benefits of small-town hospitality.

22

The Undiscovered State: Prospects for the Future

OVER GOLDEN FIELDS of wheat and corn, towns laze around on the prairie. To the visitor, North Dakota is known as a land of pheasants, ducks, hunting and fishing, blizzards, hailstorms, tornadoes, and the Badlands. Its images include the farms, ranches, small towns, vast distances, friends and family.

The state's features range from flat lakebeds (ancient Lake Agassiz formed the present-day Red River valley), to vibrant rich rolling hills, deeply carved river valleys, and step-like tablelands. The climate in the state can record the nation's hot spot in the summer or the coldest spot on any given day. Powerful blizzards and other storms can sweep across the land, covering and obliterating everything in their way.

The Missouri River divides the state into east river or west river, and the middle of the state, the "drift prairie," separates the wet region from the arid. The two designations clearly distinguish the farming environment of the east from the ranch life of the west.

Rural America has come full circle in 100 years. From vast reaches of unsettled land separated by a few trading posts to vast reaches of settled lands separated by a few population centers. From a few settlers looking for a country to a country looking for settlers. In the land of plenty, rural America is dying. The history of the land is a chronicle of a great empire that has disappeared in a trail of decaying monuments.

It is a place where you can get lost—mentally. Ultimately that is North Dakota's most powerful appeal. This is still undiscovered country. It is an empty part of the nation; the nearest lodging or meal stop may be miles away. It is a charming journey, but a bit maddening. A trip around the state is the essence of travel. It is not the destination that matters, but the adventure. It is not just a state we explored, but a state of mind.

The backcountry highways, carved by pioneers who changed the land and its culture, are the arteries through which the blood of history flows. The Western music you hear as you drive the backroads is the history of the region, and if you don't like it, open the window and hear the singing of the meadowlarks and red-winged blackbirds. These are the sounds heard from the secondary roads.

The state is one of the most misunderstood places in the United States. A large part of this misunderstanding is a result of the American people's lack of geographic knowledge and understanding of the beauty of the prairie and how solitude can enrich the soul.

This book is a sample of the 150-plus ghost towns you can see in this state, a search in several areas to see how many small towns have survived. If you visit be careful. There are nails sticking up from weathered wood. Streets are rutted. Many of the old sites are now privately owned, so it is best to ask before visiting them.

Diesel and heating oil are expensive, and rural electric rates can ruin a bank account quickly. Owner Vern Lindquist of LaVerne links two wind chargers to the existing electric system. The dual-electric system will reduce diesel fuel consumption and may serve as a prototype for future projects to harness the wind.

In this work, it is hoped that the reader has gained a new understanding of the history of this region, although with a different approach than that found in other books. The state and the towns are changing. They are figuring out there is something dramatic happening to them. It is not business as usual. The ground rules have changed, and the change can tear communities apart.

There were troubles ahead that were not visible. Most of all the structure of the rural communities characterized by much ossification produced an environment that hindered the towns' officials from meeting the challenge created by a rapidly changing economic environment. Ossification had become the hallmark. The "we've always done it this way," mentality seems pervasive.

Low-density branch lines, particularly those restricted to light rail and low-weight boxcars, were doomed. From the ashes of unwanted branch lines, a new breed of service-driven, customer-oriented regional and short lines are emerging.

Two regional (short-line) railroads have

We have super highways and super railroads. This high-speed rail line streaks across the Red River Valley landscape and stretches to infinity. More than 5,388 miles of rail lines were built in the state and most of them were straight. Jim Hill applied the rule of geometry to his Great Northern, that the shortest line between two points is a straight line.

Agriculture continues to dominate the economy. Farmers are the biggest users of rail service in the state. The state's 30,000-plus farmers produce an estimated 400 million bushels of wheat (second in the nation) and large amounts of corn, soybeans, oats, barley, rye, sugar beets and potatoes. Truly, the breadbasket of the nation, indeed the world. A Dakota, Missouri Valley & Western train passed Wilton in June 1994 with a long string of North Dakota "gold" en route to outside markets.

Baldwin does not contribute much revenue for this Dakota, Missouri Valley & Western (DMV&W) train. There is not much business in a signpost. This railroad is one of two regional rail carriers in the state. The train rolls southbound, toward Bismarck, in the summer of 1995.

The Red River Valley & Western Railroad (RRV&W), a regional carrier based in Wahpeton, serves a number of small communities in the southeast corner. The 667-mile RRVW ranks as the seventh largest of the 545 regionals and short lines operating in the U.S. The RRVW preserved essential rail service after the giant lines gave up on marginal lines, reversing a decade of downsizing. The little line has doubled its traffic volume and has helped 12 industries to locate on the line.

This string of 50 cars is at the North Central Farm Coop in Bisbee, which is the largest revenue producer on the SOO LINE's wheat line. Farmers are the biggest users of rail service in the state. Unit grain train cars remain together from origin to destination and return in a continuous conveyor belt-like cycle that is simple, efficient, and fast. You wonder why no one invented it a century ago. Elevators who could not nor would not convert to multi-car loading went out of business. On both sides of the elevator, tight against the right-of-way, are beautiful verdant blankets of grain plants, which when harvested will yield a golden flood of wheat, to be loaded in unit trains such as this and moved to market to feed a hungry world. Wheat and the elevators are the symbol of the economy of the state. The demand for grain cars is high on this day in June, 1995. Elevators are cleaning out the old crop and making ready for the new crop, only two weeks away.

Cooperation created this unit grain train. Each car on this train carries 3,500 bushels of grain, versus 1,500 in a 40-foot boxcar. The 40-foot boxcar was hurting farmers, and something had to be done. The answer was the covered hopper and the unit grain train. This train, and others like it, created large silo elevators, replacing the one-car-at-a-time shipper. It reduced freight rates, allowing farmers to compete in world markets against other grain-growing nations such as Australia, Argentina, and Canada.

"We don't want to lose the spirit of competition," said one elevator operator. "Yet we want to capitalize on cooperation and the newer grain handling methods. That is the only way we are going to survive."

formed as one solution to the grain shipping problem, which evolved as a result of the rail line abandonment program of the 1980s, a decade in which hundreds of miles of unprofitable lines were abandoned. The Red River Valley & Western, based in Wahpeton, operates more than 650 miles of former BN track in southeastern North Dakota, and the Dakota Missouri Valley & Western, based in Bismarck, operates more than 300 miles of the former SOO LINE track in the west-central part of the state. Together, the short lines serve dozens of communities, providing essential grain rail service at a freight rate the elevators can afford.

They have revitalized once-marginal operations, rekindling an enthusiasm and independent spirit not known since the original charter was granted. In the 1990s, the tracks are still there, but no longer does the commerce of the towns flow to and fro on the rails. There is only grain to haul, seasonal and subject to weather, crop failures, low prices, and dependent on an adequate rail-car supply.

Farmers are the biggest users of rail service in North Dakota. Each year the grain-gathering lines carry about 400 million bushels of wheat and a like amount of corn, barley, potatoes and sugar beets to market and processing plants.

North Dakota was a pioneer in trying to keep essential rail service when the major lines began shedding marginal branch lines. More than one-third of the towns did not survive the turbulent 1970s and 1980s. In the 1980s, it was the wholesale abandonment of branch lines in the nation, and in the 1990s it is the uncertainty, once again, that hangs over the farm belt. The new upheaval involved an orgy of mergers among the giants: Canadian Pacific/SOO LINE, Burlington Northern/Santa Fe, Union Pacific/Chicago & Northwestern, and Union Pacific/Southern Pacific.

Where this will lead is unclear, but the merger mania likely will cause fundamental changes in the policy of the grain-gathering lines. Regional lines are popping up all over. More than 300 short lines have been formed in the U.S. since the federal government gave the railroads the freedom to dump routes of little economic promise. Since 1980, when deregulation was granted, short lines have taken over some 12,000 miles of unwanted lines. The downsizing will continue; the experts predict that another 15,000 to 20,000 miles will be abandoned or spun off, and more short lines will be formed.

In the rush to downsize, the small towns first lost their depots, which were no longer needed. The 800 number replaced the local agent, then they lost the depot building, which was demolished or moved off the property. Then they lost the tracks, then the town became endangered. Lower labor costs allowed non-union short lines to make a profit on relatively little used lines and a lower carload volume. But the question remains: Can they survive?

Short lines often inherit a rundown track, and disgruntled employees and customers. They often lack the financial resources to make repairs. They usually operate with hand-me-down locomotives, rather than state-of-the-art technology. They depend on a major line for a connection and car supply, and usually depend upon one commodity: grain. One bad crop year can be disastrous.

When push comes to shove, the major lines will supply their own heavy shippers first, from which they can create the most revenue. Shippers are forced to endure the whims of the majors or they can buy their own grain cars or trucks, which they usually cannot afford. When track and locomotives wear out to a point below safe operating levels, many lines will be unable to exist.

The depot in Kenmare is no longer in use. It is a reminder of how things used to be. It stands in testimony to an earlier era when passenger trains stopped here, taking people and goods to connections and other destinations. Approximately 400 railroad stations were built in the state in a 40-year period, from 1880 to 1920. Most are gone now and only a handful remain, and have found use for other purposes (maintenance sheds), or are used by Amtrak in the larger communities.

THE DEPOT WITH NOBODY IN IT

When I walk by the railroad track,
I know the trains are not coming back.
I've passed the depot a hundred times or more,
then looking back, I know what I'm looking for.
I look inside for a ghost or two,
of the people who had work to do.
It hurts me to see windows and doors falling apart,
it's an old friend with a broken heart.

23

Last Call

WHY SHOULD AMERICANS CARE if the rural communities are dying? While the cities are growing and becoming more dense, many rural towns are moving in the opposite direction. In the next few years, the United States will pass a historical milestone: More than half of the population will live in cities and suburbs.

Rural communities are doomed! New telecommunications and better transportation have made human interaction unnecessary. The conflict between the past and the future, which fuels the cultural mix and creates urban problems, also spurs initiative, innovation, and collaboration that taken together move civilization forward.

North Dakota has done less to preserve its ghost towns than other states such as California, Nevada, or New Mexico. Ghost towns can be an important part of tourism. People like to explore, to know what they see, and to know why these places existed, and why they died. As each small town is removed, lost, defaced, or destroyed, and as they disappear, a part of history goes with them.

A note of caution is appropriate in visiting the abandoned towns. Keep in mind that the old buildings are both fragile and tinder dry. A carelessly discarded cigarette or a smoldering fire at a campsite, or any act of vandalism, may destroy these historical places forever.

It seems a shame to abandon buildings, to destroy and tear down something that could con-

tinue to be useful. A lot of people have experienced some of their most important moments in these buildings, many of which were built to last. You can't get construction like that any more. Can't a useful purpose be found for them?

"Life goes by so fast," said a museum director. "It just flashes by. People don't remember what was there before. People might not be aware of history, but it is part of the communities' character. There are hidden treasures here, from the first settlement to tracing the first stagecoach route, then later the first railroad."

Time is running out and it seems too late. Time has been working overtime, in hidden ways, unnoticed by many, recognized by too few. They are tired and listless and the "doctor" can find no physical cause or cure.

As enjoyable as our journey was, some disturbing and perplexing questions remain. Do the towns no longer have a purpose? Does anyone own them? Who owns the land on which they stand? Will calling attention to them only make them more vulnerable to vandalism, to defacing, to destruction? People must become educated to the uniqueness of the towns and their importance in history. As businesses and schools close, will the people be required to drive longer distances for the services needed, or will they abandon what is left and move? How many people will live in these towns twenty years hence?

Vestiges of another era in Cummings. Before this town went into its hibernation in the 1960s, 70s, and 80s, its population of a hundred had carved a colorful niche in the state's history. It is a idyllic setting in the Red River Valley, where the pace is slow and nobody keeps tabs on the population figures. The heart went out of the town after the businesses closed. It never reached the level of prosperity it had hoped for, and slowly and gently, it faded away.

After the town's heyday, this building went "belly up," as did several others. Many people experienced some of their most important memories in these buildings. It seems a shame that buildings were abandoned, torn down, or destroyed when they could continue to be of some use. This building was built to last; you can't get construction like this any more. Floating on a different ocean of grass, it is slowly sinking. No real boom occurred in Cummings. The population stabilized, then slipped to below ghost town status. The population figures are no longer listed on road maps, nor on road signs, even though two major highways and the BNSF Railroad serve the community.

We cannot expect others to share the same interests in the ghost towns; none the less, the prairie is worthy of attention, and cruising the combination of gravel backroads and well-maintained state roads is an interesting adventure unto itself.

If we need the quality of life offered in the rural communities, then we should take action and hang on to what is left, before the folks who call themselves "entrepreneurs" in tomorrow's histories find ways to profit from it all, and in the process destroy it.

Tourism is a gold mine, one that does not fade away. There is always a new crop of curious tourists. Ghost towns provide a sense of roots for people, a way to see the progression of their own area and a chance to see how these people had to make-do. Two hundred years from now we will be saying, "Why didn't we save these towns?" But they will be long gone. To a people hungry for depth of history, the American past is a fresh lesson for each generation. Consider the 1970s and 1980s. It was a time we thought we knew, but history is changing as we look.

Try to imagine the myriad stories behind each

The eyes of former guests of this hotel in Hixon are watching you. Inside the building vandals have made inroads. Today the arched windows gap vacantly, giving mute evidence of once plush trappings. The hotel is now decaying in gaunt emptiness. The community dates to 1909, to the building of the railroad and the establishment of a station. The floors squeak and you can hear the coyotes howl, but the hotel is not haunted. There are no rooms available at this time. No one has stayed here for a long time.

photo in this book. My fervent hope is that these images move you as much as they did me. We now have a chance through these pages to step back to the glory days and relive a special moment that many of us savored in a place that can only be North Dakota. There seems to exist in this land a complicated combination of geography, history, emotions and people. When you cross the state line and see the sign "Welcome to North Dakota," there is an immediate sense of gratification that says this is the way the world should be.

I truly wish that photos could embrace more of the human saga because certainly it's about more than just pictures. The dedication of the pioneers who built the early towns is sometimes overlooked. The individual pains and passions surely do absorb, yet we may gloss over them when looking at photos.

The past several years have been economically trying for Americans everywhere. The climate has not been favorable nor encouraging for a nostalgic review of the disappearing towns. This work is but a small chapter in the history of the rise and fall of the great prairie. Say goodbye to the ghost towns. It has been a risky and frustrating battle. They lost the fight. Enjoy this look at the past, realizing that this trip can also give you a look into the future. Thanks for taking this journey with us.

Bibliography

All photos by the author

Athearn, Robert C. *Forts of the Upper Missouri*. Lincoln: University of Nebraska Press, 1967.

Flying Diamond Publishing Co. *North Dakota, Land of Many Seasons*. North Dakota Centennial Issue. Hettinger, ND, 1989.

Gjevre, Dr. John A. *Saga of the SOO*, three volumes. Moorehead, MN: Agassiz Publishing Co., 1973, 1990, 1995.

Hart, Herbert M. *Old Forts of the Northwest*. New York: Bonanza Books, 1993.

Hegne, Barbara. *Border Outlaws of Montana, North Dakota and Canada*. Eagle Grove, OR: Published by the author, 1993.

Hidy, Ralph W., Muriel Hidy, Roy V. Scott, with Don L. Hofsommer. *Great Northern Railway—A History*. Boston: Harvard Business Press, 1988.

Houghton, Mifflin Co. *Information Please Almanac*, New York, 1995.

Iseminger, Gordon L. *Quartzite Border*. Sioux Falls, SD: Center for Western Studies, 1988.

Miller, Don E. *Ghosts on a Sea of Grass*. Missoula, MT: Pictorial Histories Publishing, Inc., 1990.

Martin, Albro. *James J. Hill and the Opening of the Northwest*. New York: Oxford Press, 1976.

McKeon, Jacaure. *If That Don't Beat the Devil*. Rochester, NY: American Baptist Society, 1985.

Mitchell, Stewart. *Midland Continental, A History*. Milwaukee, WI: Kalmbach Publishing Co., 1972.

McWhither, Norris and Ross. *Guinness Book of World Records*. New York: Sterling Publishing Co., 1993.

National Railway Publishing Co. *Official Guide of the Railways*. New York, June, 1968.

Razetta, Helen Graham. *The Making of the Two Dakotas*. Lincoln, NE: Media Publishing Co., 1988.

Renz, Louis Tuck. *History of the Northern Pacific*. Fairfield, WA: Ye Galleon Press, 1980.

Taylor, Norman and Wilma. *America's Chapel Cars*. Pasadena, CA: Locomotive and Railway Preservation Magazine, December, 1996.

Wick, Douglas A. *North Dakota Place Names*. Bismarck, ND: Hedemarken Collectibles, 1988.

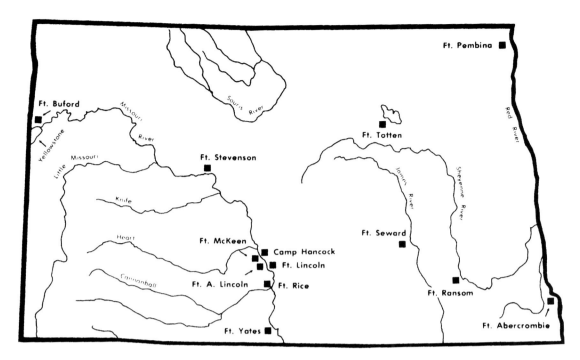

River systems and forts of North Dakota

North Dakota Statistics

State Capital	Bismarck, 1990 population: 49,256
Highest point	White Butte, near Amidon, 3,506 feet
Lowest point	Pembina, upper Red River Valley, 750 feet
Population	652,695 population in 1990, 46th in nation
Width	360.5 miles east to west
Length	210 miles south to north
Area	70,685 square miles, 17th in nation
Location	Geographical center of continent, at Rugby
Border markers	46th parallel, with South Dakota, 720 quartzite markers
Number of counties	53
Number of post offices	484
Smallest county	Eddy, 642 square miles
Largest county	McKenzie, 2,768 square miles
Smallest population	Slope County, 1990 population: 900, 1,226 square miles
Largest population	Cass County, 1990 population: 102,874
Largest City	Fargo, 1990 population: 74,111
Smallest town	Hove's Mobile Park City, 1990 population: 2
Longest River	Red River, on eastern border, 545 river miles
Miles of railroad track	5,388 miles
Number of rail sites	670 hamlets, villages, towns and cities served by rail.

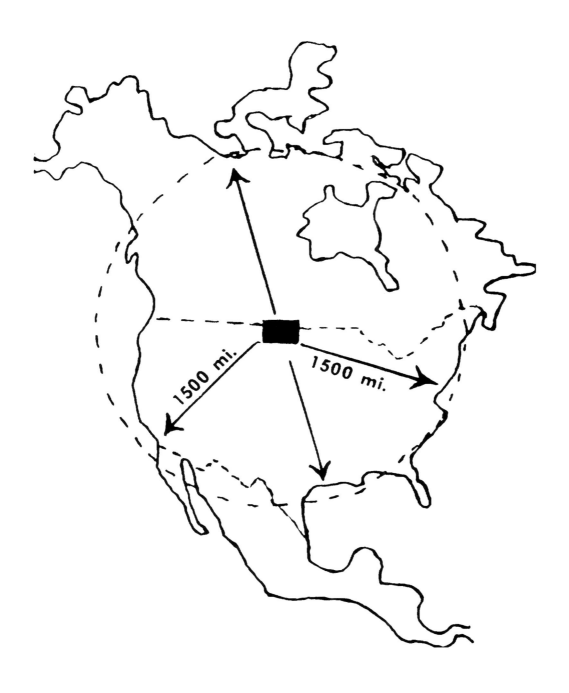

Geographical Location

North Dakota is the geographical center of North America.
A monument at Rugby marks the exact spot.

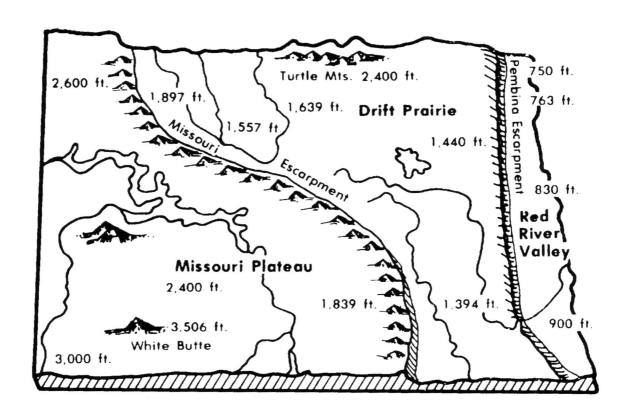

The following elevations appear on the illustration:

- 2,600 ft.
- 1,897 ft.
- 1,557 ft.
- Turtle Mts. 2,400 ft.
- 1,639 ft.
- **Drift Prairie**
- 1,440 ft.
- Missouri Escarpment
- 750 ft.
- 763 ft.
- Pembina Escarpment
- 830 ft.
- **Red River Valley**
- **Missouri Plateau** 2,400 ft.
- 3,506 ft. White Butte
- 3,000 ft.
- 1,839 ft.
- 1,394 ft.
- 900 ft.

Three Broad Steps

Like giant steps North Dakota's terrain rises from the level Red River Valley, elevation 750 feet above sea level and once a glacial lake, then steadily rises to the west 300 to 400 feet to the central drift prairie, then another 300 to 400 feet to the Missouri River escarpment. West of the river it climbs again into the slope country, rising to 3,506 feet at White Butte.

Rainfall and snowpack have created their own drainage systems, and have long ago broken through into the river systems. Drainage is poor; the river systems do not always handle the onrushing waters. Flooding, particularly in the Red River Valley, is common. Weather patterns tend to follow the diagonal lay of the land, and sudden rain storms can drop additional water into the rivers. Western ranchers who want to conserve water must build containment dams.

North Dakota's Railway Systems in the Early 1900s

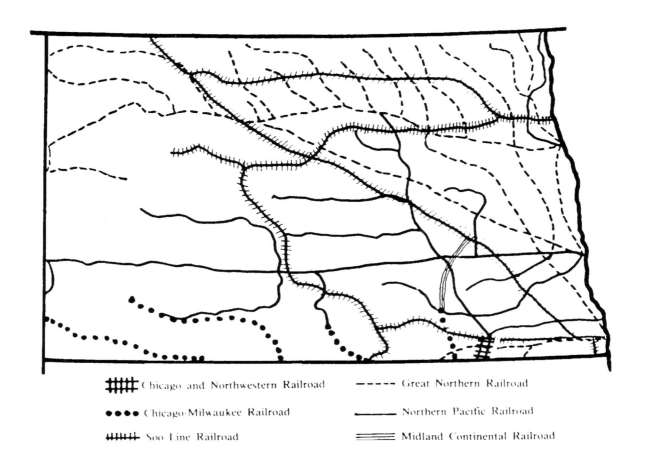

┼┼┼┼ Chicago and Northwestern Railroad		- - - - Great Northern Railroad	
●●●● Chicago-Milwaukee Railroad		——— Northern Pacific Railroad	
┼┼┼┼┼ Soo Line Railroad		≡≡≡ Midland Continental Railroad	

Index to Counties, Cities, and Railway Stations

About the Author

KEN BROVALD spent his growing up years in northern North Dakota, on a cattle/grain ranch along the main line of the then Great Northern Railroad and U.S. Highway No. 2. His interest in the subject and the people runs deep. The exposure to the small towns stimulated a lifelong interest in the state and the rural towns.

He has written one book and has published several magazine articles. This book is on a subject long overlooked by historians and photographers. He currently writes a monthly column for a railroad club. Ken is retired, which allows him more time for research, traveling, photography, and writing. He lives in Anchorage, Alaska, with his wife, Arlene, who also has deep roots in North Dakota and shares this interest.